COSPLAY
Casey Welsch

FOUNDATIONS

Your Guide to Constructing Bodysuits,
Corsets, Hoop Skirts, Petticoats & More

FanPoweredPRESS
IMAGINE | MAKE | BECOME

Text and photography copyright © 2022 by Casey Welsch

Artwork copyright © 2022 by C&T Publishing, Inc.

Publisher: Amy Barrett-Daffin

Creative Director: Gailen Runge

Senior Editor: Roxane Cerda

Editor: Beth Baumgartel

Technical Editor: Helen Frost

Cover Book Designer: April Mostek

Production Coordinator: Zinnia Heinzmann

Production Editor: Jennifer Warren

Illustrator: Mary E. Flynn

Photography Coordinator: Lauren Herberg

Photography Assistant: Gabriel Martinez

Published by FanPowered Press, an imprint of C&T Publishing, Inc.,
P.O. Box 1456, Lafayette, CA 94549

Library of Congress Cataloging-in-Publication Data

Names: Welsch, Casey, 1989- author.

Title: Cosplay foundations : your guide to constructing bodysuits, corsets,
    hoop skirts, petticoats & more / Casey Welsch of Casey Renee Cosplay.

Description: Lafayette : FanPowered Press, [2022] | Summary: "Includes
    step-by-step instructions to create a full set of foundation garments
    that can be mixed and matched to create the perfect just-for-you
    silhouette for any cosplay you build"-- Provided by publisher.

Identifiers: LCCN 2021062220 | ISBN 9781644031957 (trade paperback) | ISBN
    9781644031964 (ebook)

Subjects: LCSH: Costume. | Cosplay.

Classification: LCC TT633 .W45 2022 | DDC 646.4/78--dc23/eng/20220201

LC record available at https://lccn.loc.gov/2021062220

Printed in the USA

10 9 8 7 6 5 4 3 2

⁓ *Dedication*

Thanks to my dog turned house elf, Eva, for stealing my socks and for sneaking into every shot of a finished piece.

To my partner and best friend Toby, for keeping me sane, cooking meals when deadlines were coming up, and having dance parties in my sewing studio when I was having writer's block. You are the only exception.

To my stepmom Lois, who tried to teach me how to sew when I was twelve. When we got the pattern cut out and I lost complete interest, she let me continue in my chaotic way by safety pinning it all together. To this day I stand behind the fashion decisions of a twelve-year-old me.

To my Dad for reminding me that I won't know until I try.

To all my friends and family who stand by me through all the missed events and who allow me to bring my hand sewing everywhere I go. You encourage and inspire me daily to keep making my dreams a reality.

ACKNOWLEDGMENTS

I could not have done this without Alex Brumley from Alexandra Lee Studios and the fantastic photos that she brought to this book. Also, a very special thank you to Amanda Hass for holding my hand through this process and assuring me every step of the way that I can do this. To quote the wickedest witch I know, "We are led to those who help us most to grow, if we let them." Thank you, Alex and Amanda, for helping me grow into the person and artist I am today; you both have changed me for good.

A huge thank you to the entire team at C&T Publishing who helped me turn my love and passion for undergarments into something that will help others love them too.

CONTENTS

INTRODUCTION

In the last few years, cosplay has grown exponentially in popularity. With the growth of the Marvel Cinematic Universe, the Star Wars Universe, and with thousands of video games released every year, there is so much content to cosplay from. Cosplayers are not only pulling from these sources, but books and D&D (Dungeons and Dragons). Original characters are becoming incredibly popular to cosplay as well. As cosplay becomes more mainstream, cosplayers work even harder to level up their craftsmanship and creativity. Finding the exact garments to piece together a cosplay through thrifting and online shopping is an art form in and of itself. However, there is a rather large movement towards construction. As the world changes and resources become more widely available, costume construction is more accessible, and I am so excited to help you learn about the beauty and shape of cosplay undergarments.

Have you ever been standing on the convention floor, posing for pictures, or chatting with friends, and a cosplayer walks by with a costume that leaves you speechless? Every detail from how their armor seamlessly pieces together, or how their layers of skirts float as they walk, or even the way they carry themselves as if their wings were an extension of their body is spellbinding.

Chances are, those cosplayers are wearing foundation garments, like a spandex bodysuit, a hoop skirt, or a corset. There is so much that goes into making a costume and so much that goes on underneath a costume to make it look professional. Like the foundation of a building, the garment or set of garments can be the key to creating elaborate costumes with many moving parts. A properly fitted set of foundation garments can help take the World of Warcraft character out of Azeroth and make it come alive in our world.

Undergarments often help make the pieces of a costume come together that might not make sense on paper or in a video game. They can help create a dramatic silhouette for a costume and bring showmanship to a Masquerade Stage. Engineering the proper movement for armor and ballgowns is possible with a well-made set of foundation garments.

In the following chapters, I will give you the tools you need to create your very own undergarments. I will provide you with tips and tricks to create well-made, long-lasting, and interchangeable garments. Ultimately there is no right or wrong way to sew; the instructions and tips provided come from my own experiences. Cosplay construction is an art form, and if you are anything like me, self-expression will permeate through everything you make.

COSPLAYER: Casey Renee
COSTUME: Sakizou Amethyst
from Sakizou Artworks

Photography by Alexandra Lee Studios

ABOUT FOUNDATION GARMENTS

A *foundation garment* is any garment worn underneath clothing that has a function or a purpose. In modern fashion, a white cotton shirt under a three-piece suit is considered a foundation garment, as is a satin slip under a dress. Foundation garments have various functions, but their sole purpose is to make wearing the outer garments easier, more comfortable, and create a silhouette. They serve to shield the clothes from sweat or protect the wearer from scratchy fabrics. While there are staple foundation garments like the corset, spandex bodysuit, and hoop skirt, each of these basic garments can change dramatically to adapt to the wearer's needs and the type of costume.

Foundation garments are also a key factor for any cosplayer making the leap to creating competition-level cosplays. It's common practice in top-tier competitions to create every garment possible. Having the ability to sew your knee-length leggings means you can customize them to look exactly like the anime character in mind. Everything, including the fuku or bodysuit Sailor Moon wears, can become customized to the size and shape of the wearer.

Creating a set of hoops and a corset can give a cosplayer the silhouette on which to drape ball gowns, from Belle to Princess Peach! Unlocking ball gown undergarments allows the cosplayer to turn their favorite characters from Baymax to Iron Man into a ball gown. Just one knee-length petticoat can support the creation of dozens of characters and can even be worn under 1950's dresses to give them more poof.

COSPLAYER: Casey Renee Cosplay
COSTUME: Ariel from *The Little Mermaid*
Photography by Toby Johnson

COSPLAYER: Casey Renee Cosplay

COSTUME: Rococo Belle based on
Belle from *Beauty and the Beast*

Photography by Alexandra Lee Studios

Foundation Garments Throughout History

History can inform us on what undergarments work best for cosplay. Historically, undergarments were layered. Instead of just a shirt, there would be a shirt, then a quilted tunic, followed by leather or metal armor. This combination of undergarments gave a warrior comfort and safety while fighting, and then once the fighting was finished and the armor removed, the warrior could sleep in the undergarments and be warm and protected from the elements. Likewise, women like Marie Antoinette often layered a chemise, stays, pockets, pannier, and petticoats under a *robe à la francaise* (gown) to create a desired silhouette. As cosplayers, we get to mix and match and use what we know about these undergarments to develop silhouettes for characters that may or may not have ever existed in the real world.

The first pair of underwear dates as far back as 1300 BC. The "loincloth" was a triangular linen piece of fabric often worn by Egyptian workers in the Bronze Age. Pharaoh Tutankhamun was known to have worn a goatskin loincloth and was buried with 145 spare loincloths to bring into the afterlife with him. Leather and linen loincloths were worn

by gladiators in ancient Rome, while Roman women typically wore a band around their breasts called a *stropium*.

As far back as the seventh century, Japanese warriors wore a padded undergarment under their lamellar, or plated, armor. In Medieval times, chainmail was often worn under armor. These garments protected the wearers from the stiff leather, metal, or even stone used to create the armor. These undergarments were also easier to wash and to take care of than the armor itself. They could even keep the wearer warm.

In the thirteenth century, garments like the gambeson and the shift had double purposes. The gambeson, a padded jacket, doubled as armor or it could be worn beneath the armor to prevent chafing. Women often wore a shift, or chemise, closest to their skin for comfort, warmth, and to protect the outer garment from sweat. The chemise has evolved quite a bit over time and by the 1930s they became slip-style dresses!

The undergarments worn by women changed dramatically during the sixteenth century. What was worn to a ball in 1680 changed dramatically by 1780. Corsets and hoops continued to evolve into the nineteenth century. We'll talk more about corsets and hoops later in this book, and how these two garments alone can create all kinds of illusions. Since garments like cage crinolines were worn like clothes, we as cosplayers can learn from historical construction how to make something suitable for Cinderella to wear to a ball.

Tudor-era large bum roll

Corsets and padding were (and are) also used to alter silhouettes and to create the illusion of being a different gender or genderless all together. Drag queens use tights and padding to create a feminine figure, just like women in the Victorian era used padding to form the illusion of a tiny waist. The modern development of elastic has made it possible to produce garments that compress breasts to create the illusion of a flatter chest. Padding the shoulders and upper arms of a garment would create the triangular figure that historically men often desired.

Today, you can wear shapewear and bras under form-fitting dresses to emphasize silhouette and hide unwanted curves. Cotton shirts are worn underneath suits to absorb sweat and keep suits cleaner longer.

COSPLAYER: Sudanrobladeworks

COSTUME: The Witcher from *The Witcher*

Photography by Alexandra Lee Studios

COSPLAYER: Malicious_K Cosplay
COSTUME: Zelda from *Legend of Zelda*
Photography by Alexandra Lee Studios

Foundation Garments in Cosplay

Like most aspects of cosplay, foundation garments can be as creative as the costumer making the costume. They can be adapted for you and your vision! The basic and most popular foundation garments for cosplay are corsets, hoop skirts, petticoats, shifts, bloomers, bodysuits, leggings, shorts, and wristlets, and all are covered in this book.

For foundation garments to be fully effective and to function better, there are suggested materials and closures for each garment. Each piece created to go under all the fancy bits of your costume should serve both you and your costume and not just exist to exist. You can decide that you don't need a corset and that a fully-boned bodice is perfect. It is your cosplay!

There are no limitations to how you can use foundation garments. A Sailor Scout fuku can be used for any costume that requires alternating parts like skirts and bows; they can even be worn under armor as a base for some costumes.

Bodysuits also help with armor placement and help keep the pieces from slipping around on the body. And, remember a bodysuit for under a set of armor doesn't have to be made in basic black, it can be techno-colored, or even airbrushed. It can also have hidden pockets for batteries or cooling packs, and Velcro or magnets for securing armor or capes,

Spandex garments like shorts and leggings can also live double lives. Shorts are perfect under short skirts or in fur suits. Leggings can replace bloomers if comfort is more important than frills.

Hoops and corsets can work together to help distribute the weight of a ballgown.

Cage crinoline

COSPLAYER: Casey Renee Cosplay

COSTUME: Original design inspired by
Sally Skellington from *The Nightmare
Before Christmas*

Photography by Toby Johnson

FABRICS, NOTIONS, BONING, AND TOOLS

Fabrics

Fabrics are just the beginning—for many foundation garments they are the "foundation" upon which the garment is built! Natural fibers like cotton and silk make amazing fabric choices for ballgown undergarments. Synthetic fabrics like Lycra and spandex are great for underneath armor. There are so many fabrics to choose from!

Cotton Fabrics

You can use cotton fabrics for much more than just your grandma's quilts. Cotton is easy to sew with minimal fraying or slipping and is machine washable. It can be pressed with an iron or steamed and is very comfortable on a hot summer day. Use universal needles in size 80/12 when sewing on cotton.

PRINTED QUILTERS COTTON is a lovely fabric to work into the outer garments on cosplay, but different types of cotton can be game changers for undergarments.

BROADCLOTH, a medium-weight, plain-weave cotton, is ideal for shifts and bloomers. For undergarments such as bloomers, 100% cotton fabric is best since it makes it easier for the body to breathe.

COTTON LAWN is a lightweight, high-thread-count cotton that is slightly sheer and is perfect for a chemise or bloomers. The handkerchief feeling of this material makes it soft to the skin and very breathable under all the layers of costume. As long as the fabric is washed before you cut it out, it can also be washed after it's turned into the perfect garment.

Broadcloth

Cotton lawn

Blouse: cotton lawn;
skirt: polyester satin

COUTIL is a densely woven fabric with a herringbone weave invented in the 1800s for corset making. Coutil can be found in 100% cotton, polyester, or a poly-cotton blend and is available in a variety of weights. The best coutil for corsetry is 100% cotton because it breathes.

DENIM is an excellent alternative for coutil. It is a strong fabric constructed in a twill weave. Traditionally denim was woven with a 100% cotton yarn in indigo and white that, when woven, created the blue hue we commonly see. Modern denim can be made from polyester and polyblend yarn in various colors and prints and is widely available at local fabric shops.

Coutil

TIP

Both coutil and denim are easy to sew using a strong, durable needle. Use a universal needle in size 90/14 for light- and medium-weight fabrics and a 100/16 needle for heavier weight fabrics. You can also use a denim/jeans needle.

Silk Fabrics

Silk fibers make great fashion fabric for corsets. Silk is a strong, lustrous fiber produced by silkworms. It can be woven in several ways to create different types of silk that all have their preferred uses. Silk made from pre-dyed thread is best used unwashed. Otherwise, the dyes can bleed, and it will ruin the two-tone effect. Three types of silk stand out for fashion fabric in undergarments: dupioni, taffeta, and shantung.

TIP

All silk should be sewn with silk-specific needles such as microtext sharp needles in sizes 70/10, 80/12, or 90/14, depending on the weight of the fabric. Silk is prone to fraying, so overlocking or edge finishing the fabric early in the process will make sewing it much easier.

SILK DUPIONI is a plain weave, crisp fabric with fine thread in the warp and uneven thread in the weft. These two threads are often different colors creating a two-tone iridescent effect. Dupioni is similar to shantung but is slightly thicker and heavier.

SILK SHANTUNG is similar to dupioni with fine thread in the warp and the uneven thread in the weft. Since the weft thread is more even, shantung has less texture and is lighter weight than dupioni.

SILK TAFFETA is a high-end fabric with a plain weave that is crisp and smooth, almost paper-like. Yarn-dyed silk taffeta is commonly used in ball gowns and corsetry. It also has a two-toned effect and requires a bit more attention than silk dupioni and silk shantung. Since it is so smooth and crisp, sewing needles need to be sharp and changed often. Silk pins or wonder clips are the best options when sewing, and if pins are used, place them in the seam allowances or holes may be visible in the garment.

Silk dupioni

Silk shantung

Silk taffeta

COSPLAYER: Casey Renee Cosplay
COSTUME: Eighteenth-century pumpkin dress
Photography by Toby Johnson

Linen

Linen is a strong and absorbent fiber made from flax plants. It is great for chemise and under-shirts, and it is soft, comfortable to wear, and dries faster than cotton. Linen can be found in many different weights, but **LIGHTWEIGHT HANDKER-CHIEF LINEN** is best for undergarments due to the many layers of cosplay costumes.

Lightweight handkerchief linen

Tulle and Organza

TULLE is made with various fibers such as polyester, nylon, or silk. It is a lightweight, fine net
fabric, traditionally used for bridal veils, and is
great for petticoats, tutus, or even ballgowns.
Tulle is available in a variety of colors and
widths and sold by the yard or, more economi-
cally, by the bolt. Since it is a net fabric, tulle
doesn't fray, but don't let that fool you, it still
can be difficult to sew.

Sewing with tulle can be tricky for the first
time. Here are a few tips to help!

- Add a piece of transparent tape to the bottom
  of the presser foot to help the net glide
  through your machine easier.

- Use a zig-zag stitch or the longest stitch
  length (4mm) on your sewing machine.

- Safety pin the pieces together so you don't
  accidentally lose pins in the bulk of the fabric;
  just be sure to safety pin away from the edge
  of the fabric so you can breeze past them
  while sewing.

Another amazing fabric for petticoats is **ORGANZA**:
a thin, sheer, plain weave fabric made of silk,
polyester, or nylon. Organza is softer than tulle.
Crystal organza makes beautiful petticoats, and
mixing colors of organza can create amazing
effects for dancing or twirling. Organdy is the
cotton variation of organza, and the crisp-
ness creates a lovely stiffness but is prone to
wrinkles.

- To minimize fraying for organza, lightly burn
  the edge of the fabric piece right after cutting
  it; a hot knife is the best tool for this.

- Use a long stitch length, and a microtex sharp
  needle in size 70/10, to help minimize puckering. Avoid universal needles since they will
  pull at the fibers.

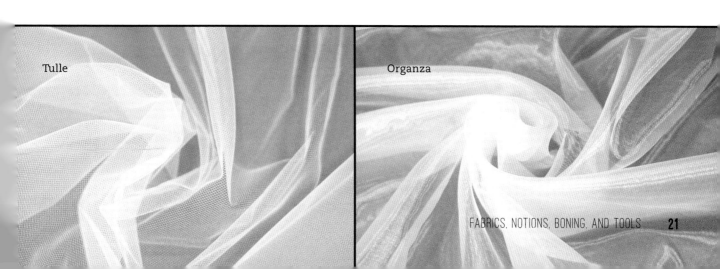

Tulle

Organza

Spandex/Lycra

LYCRA, commonly referred to as **SPANDEX**, is a synthetic fiber known for its ability to stretch. This elasticity is perfect for bodysuits, fukus, leggings, corset covers, or anything that needs to be fitted to the body while allowing the body to have a wide range of motion. Spandex comes in 2-way and 4-way stretch; the 4-way stretch is the desired choice for bodysuits and leggings so you can get the optimal amount of movement in your costume.

Working with spandex is its own kind of monster to slay! Since the fabric stretches it's very important to make sure the seams and finishes can stretch with it. There are several ways to do this.

- Use a jersey or ballpoint needle. This will help the machine from dropping the stitches.

- A *zigzag stitch* is a fantastic stitch found on most sewing machines. It works great for sewing spandex, however, not so great if the spandex needs to stretch. The stitch leaves gaps in between each zag and that can cause tears. This stitch slightly puckers the fabric so the garment seams might not always have the best look, but it is completely acceptable.

- The *overcast stitch* is another option. This stitch is great for seaming and finishing the edge of garments. It lays flatter than the zigzag and since it is a three-part stitch it's extremely durable.

- Some machines also have the *lightning bolt stitch*, which is a zigzag stitch with both short and long stitches and looks like a lightning bolt. This stitch lays flatter than the zigzag and tends to minimize puckering.

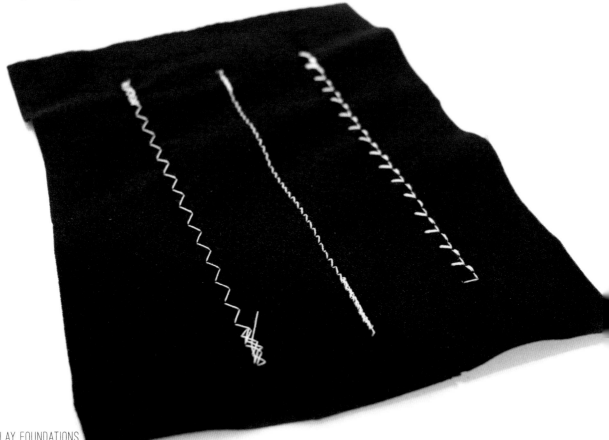

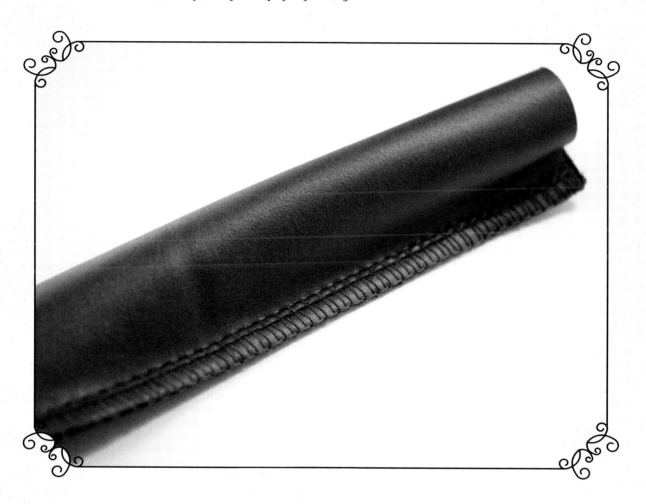

Fabric Amounts

Instead of exact yardage, usually a range of yardage amounts are listed with each project. The exact amount to purchase depends on the size of the garment you will be making and the width of the fabric you will be using. Not only do different fabrics come in different widths, but sometimes the same fabric is available in different widths. Most cotton fabric is about 44″ (1.2m) wide but silk shantung can be found in this width as well as 54″ (1.4m) wide. Fashion fabrics will vary in width but organza and spandex are consistently 60″ (1.5m) wide as is coutil for corsets at 54″ (1.4m) wide. Wait to purchase the fashion fabric for your project until you've done the measuring and pattern prep described in the projects.

Notions and Boning

Boning Basics for Corsets and Hoops

A major material that creates the structure for both hoop skirts and corsets is a material called boning. Historically, natural materials like reed and whale bone were used in these undergarments. While reed is still available for boning, options such as whale bone became scarce, so other materials took its place. Sometimes even steel and hard wood was used to make busks (a rigid element in the center front) for corsets.

STEEL BONING FOR CORSETS

Steel is a very common material used for both corset boning and busks. It is incredibly strong and can be formed into many thicknesses and widths for the purpose of boning. The two major types of steel boning are flat steel and spiral steel. Both can be purchased in precut lengths as well as a continuous roll. Boning purchased in a continuous roll does require metal cutters and boning caps to create clean boning ends and prevent the boning from popping out of the corset.

FLAT STEEL BONING can only move two directions which makes it ideal for reinforcing the center front and back of corsets especially when placed next to grommets. An extra wide piece of flat steel boning is a great replacement for a busk when in a pinch.

SPIRAL STEEL BONING can bend on all sides without bending out of shape. Spiral steel is both strong and flexible and is an amazing choice for the curves of a corset. For those looking for a tighter laced corset, spiral steel is the best option for the job. Spiral steel can be cut with metal cutters. To create a clean edge, Plasti Dip coating is a great option, as well as heat shrink tubing made for plumbing.

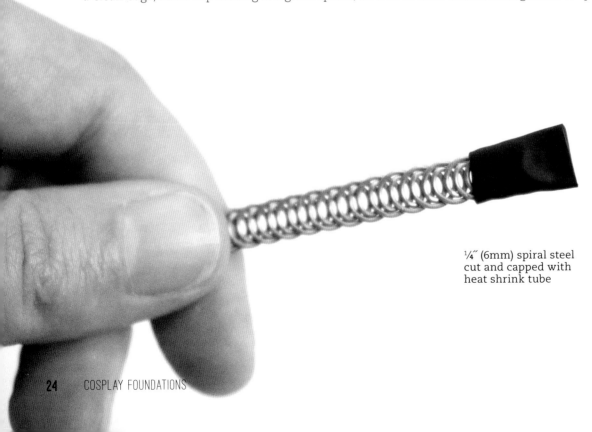

¼˝ (6mm) spiral steel cut and capped with heat shrink tube

COSPLAYER:
Casey Renee Cosplay

Costume: Tudor chemise, stays,
farthingale, and bum roll

*Photography by
Alexandra Lee Studios*

SYNTHETIC BONING FOR CORSETS

SYNTHETIC WHALE BONE is made to act exactly like whale bone and it is an excellent choice for historical corsetry. Synthetic whale bone comes in multiple widths as a continuous roll or by individual lengths. This option can be used to replace spiral steel if desired.

PLASTIC BONING is a medium strength boning, great for stays. It is not great for reduction on a corset, so if tight lacing or waist training is the goal then plastic boning might not be the best option. Plastic boning can be bought on a continuous roll, which might help save some money, and can be cut with sharp craft scissors.

TIP *Boning can be expensive, so make your wallet love you by using zip ties when making a mock-up. You'll get exact measurements and know exactly how much you need to buy of the more expensive corset boning.*

STEEL BUSKS FOR CORSETS

A **SPLIT BUSK** forms the front closure of a corset. Historically they were not split and were made of metal or wood. Modern split busks are made of flat steel and provide extra stability at the front of a corset. Narrow flexible busks are commonly used and come in lengths varying from 7″ to 18″ (17.8 to 45.7cm) and in multiple color combinations. Heavy-duty busks are used for both modern and Victorian-style corsets; they come in varying colors and lengths, but they create a straighter front profile than narrow flexible busks.

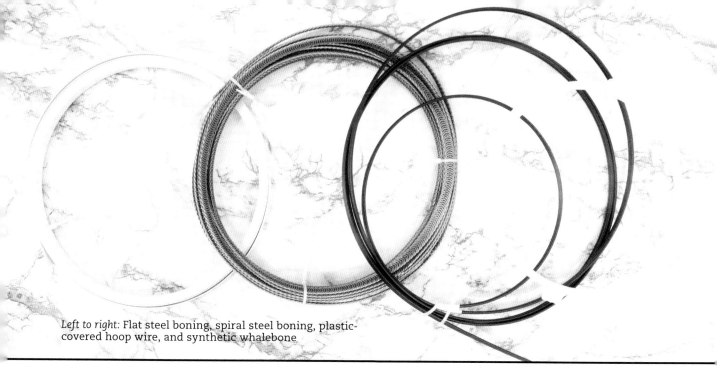

Left to right: Flat steel boning, spiral steel boning, plastic-covered hoop wire, and synthetic whalebone

CRINOLINE BONING AND BONE CASING

Crinolines and hoop skirts have a couple of boning options as well. The first is *steel hoop boning*, which feels and acts quite a bit like flat steel boning for corsets but only comes in a continuous roll and in ¼″ (7mm) and ½″ (13mm) widths.

PLASTIC-COVERED HOOP WIRE is made up of two wires running parallel to each other encased in plastic. It is lightweight and very strong; it takes quite a bit to bend it out of shape and is honestly the best boning if you want to make the one crinoline to rule them all!

BONE CASING is a fabric casing to hold the boning. It comes in a couple of different sizes to suit the size of the boning. Bone casing is easy to sew and makes attaching the hoops easy and helps create a more flexible hoop skirt.

Fishing Line and Twill Tape

FISHING LINE is very handy for sewing into the hem of a petticoat. It's nearly invisible when sewn into a rolled hem (page 33) and gives a magical gravity-defying look to the petticoat that also allows it to support the dress over it.

TWILL TAPE is a sturdy strip of fabric that is woven with a diagonal line pattern; it comes in many widths and is very strong. Twill tape can be used in binding edges such as the waist of a petticoat or the bottom of a corset. It is also be used in hoop skirts as the perpendicular tape that holds the boning wire to the hoop.

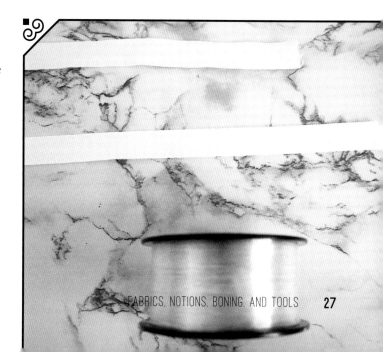

Tools

There are several specialty tools that are helpful with the sewing of foundation garments.

A **GROMMET SETTING KIT** is helpful for placing metal grommets in corsets. Grommets are two-part metal eyelets that make a great closure for bodices and corsets. They come in many sizes and colors. A grommet setting kit includes grommets typically in a single size (but some come with multiple sizes), two metal tools for installing the top and bottom pieces of the grommet, and a rubber mallet to enclose the grommet around the fabric.

An **AWL** is a small, pointed tool used for piercing holes. It can be useful making the hole in the fabric prior to installing the grommet pieces. An awl can also be useful for leatherworking or with heavy materials.

METAL CUTTERS are the best tool for cutting both spiral steel and hoop wire.

WONDER CLIPS are a game changer when trying to hold hoop wire onto the structure of your hoop. They are little clips that can hold layers of fabric together and unlike pins they do not puncture your fabric. Since you can't pin through steel, clipping it is the next best alternative until you can sew the areas around it.

Left to right: Hole punch, mallet, awl, grommet setting tools, and grommets

Ruffler foot (*left*); gathering foot (*right*)

There are three **SPECIALTY PRESSER FEET** that all basically help aid in the process of petticoat making. All three feet are not necessary, just pick the foot that suits you. The three feet are a walking foot, ruffler foot, and a gathering foot.

A **WALKING FOOT** is used when sewing lots of layers of fabric together; it is like having a top set of feed dogs to help feed fabric through the machine. The foot is rather bulky and can be very tricky to put on the sewing machine, but it is useful for sewing lots of different types of fabric especially heavyweight ones.

A **RUFFLER FOOT** is another bulky sewing machine foot that is perfect for gathering fabric and making ruffles. Most ruffler feet have several settings on the foot to help determine the length and amount of fabric that will be ruffled in each stitch. Ruffler feet can be a bit tricky to use at first and need to be tested each time you change your fabric type because the tension will vary.

The **GATHERING FOOT** is a lot smaller than walking and ruffler feet and is great for creating even gathers in fabric. A gathering foot works best with lightweight materials and is not suitable for gathering heavier materials. The gathers created from a gathering foot are softer than those created with a ruffler foot.

CONSTRUCTION SKILLS

Pattern Prep

Not all cosplay foundation garments require a pattern, however some are much easier to sew with the guidance of a pattern. Full-size downloads of patterns for the corset, bloomers, and cowl are available; each of those projects will contain the link.

DOWNLOADABLE PATTERNS

You can download full-size patterns for the corset, bloomers, and cowl at

tinyurl.com/11481-patterns-download.

Once you download and print the patterns it's time to transfer them to fabric. Before you cut any fabric decide whether you want to make a mock-up. I highly recommend making one, especially of the corset, to ensure perfect fit. Make the mock-ups using less expensive fabric but similar weight and fiber content of the fashion fabric.

If you are between sizes, it's best to make your garment the larger size because you can always take things in. I suggest cutting out the largest pattern size close to your measurements. Mark the pattern size you plan to use by drawing an "x" periodically on the cutting lines.

Press the pattern pieces flat, using a low heat setting. Also press your fabrics, using the appropriate heat setting. Place the pattern pieces onto the wrong side of your fabric, pin them in place, and cut along the edges. Be sure to cut out the notches too, to make matching the pieces easier during sewing. Finally, use transfer paper and a tracing wheel to transfer any construction markings.

Pattern transfer paper and tracing wheel

COSPLAYER: Jedimanda
COSTUME: Princess Anastasia from *Anastasia*

Photography by Alexandra Lee Studios

Machine Stitching

Basic sewing skills are necessary for most cosplay sewing. Much of the sewing can be done by machine. A basic straight stitch is suitable for the woven fabrics, however stretch fabrics do require sewing with a stitch that stretches too.

Stretch Stitches

ZIGZAG STITCH is a back-and-forth stitch used to sew knit fabrics such as spandex and to clean finish the edge of woven fabric.

OVERCAST STITCH requires an overcast presser foot that has a bar in the center so that the thread wraps around the edge of the fabric as you stitch.

LIGHTNING BOLT STITCH is a variation of the zigzag stitch. It should be set at 2mm wide and 2.5mm long. This narrow stitch permits the seam to be pressed completely flat.

Stitch Length

Most of the projects in this book require a 2.5mm stitch length.

SHORT STITCH LENGTH is between .5–1.5mm.

LONG STITCH LENGTH ranges between 3.5–5mm.

BASTING stitches are 4mm or longer. Some machines have a basting stitch programmed into the machine so check your manual to see if yours does.

Seams

Most of the projects in this book require a basic seam, however for sheer fabrics or fabrics that ravel, some specialty seams are helpful.

The **FRENCH SEAM** is one of the easiest seams to create a clean finish inside the garment.

- Sew the fabric pieces with *wrong* sides together using a scant ½″ (12mm) seam allowance.

- Trim the seam allowance to ⅛″ (3mm).

- Fold the fabric with *right* sides together, making sure the first seam is at the very edge, and press.

- Stitch ¼″ (12mm) from the folded edge of the fabric, encasing the raw edges. **figs A & B**

An **OVERLOCK SEAM** requires a stitch that sews over the edges of the fabric while joining the pieces together. An overlock machine even trims the raw edges of the fabric while it stitches the seam. **fig C**

UNDERSTITCHING is a way to keep a seam allowance from rolling toward the outside of the garment. It is sewn close to the inside edge of the lining or facing, often at a neckline. After stitching the seam, press the seam allowance toward the lining or facing, and clip or notch the seam allowance if necessary. Stitch on the lining or facing layer, about ⅛″ to ¼″ (3.1 to 6mm) from the seam. Press the lining or facing toward the inside of the garment. **fig D**

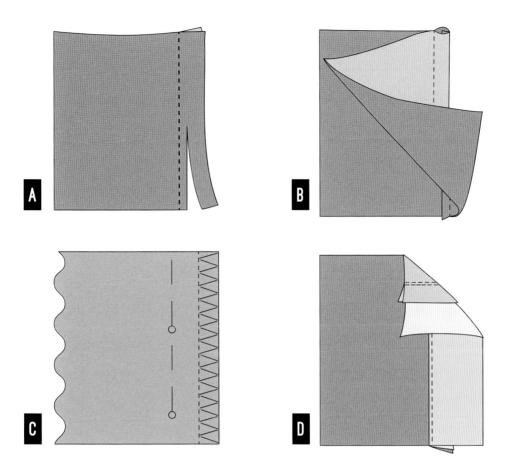

Hems

To sew a basic **FOLDED HEM**, fold the fabric ½″ (12mm) to the wrong side and press. Fold the fabric another ½″ (12mm), and press again. Stitch next to the folded edge.

To sew a hem on stretch fabrics such as spandex, fold the fabric ½″ (12mm) to the wrong side and press. It's not necessary to make a second fold; sew next to the raw edge using a stretch stitch.

A **ROLLED HEM** is a tiny hem that is perfect for light to medium-weight fabrics. To sew rolled hems, you need a rolled hem presser foot in size ⅛″ or 2mm. This foot has a funnel-shaped coil that makes the fabric edge turn under twice as you sew. Place the fabric right side down and sew a few stitches. Guide the fabric into the coil using the thread tails to help pull the fabric into place. Use a straight stitch and sew slowly to keep the fabric feeding into the foot.

To add fishing line (page 27), to a rolled hem, guide the fabric into the coil then guide the fishing line through the center of the rolled section. Feed the fishing line through to the other side of the foot with the thread tails. Sew using a narrow zigzag stitch to encase the fishing line. Trim the ends of the fishing line once the hem is finished.

Hand Stitching

Most of the sewing for the foundation garments is done by machine, but sometimes hand stitching is necessary, and it tends to add a fine finishing touch. Some historical costume makers, those who go to the lengths of sewing garments as they did in the era they were worn, make the entire garment by hand. For this book we are going to stick to more modern practices, however several of the featured tips and techniques are useful if you ever want to take a more historical approach.

Backstitch

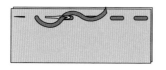

The back stitch is a strong stitch because the thread on the back of the work overlaps two stitches at a time. To create this stitch, bring the needle to the front of the fabric and make one stitch back toward the right. Bring up the needle to the left of the first stitch and make another stitch to the right, putting the needle back through the hole where the first stitch ended, then bringing the needle back to the front of the fabric. Continue working from right to left, making the stitches the same size.

Catchstitch

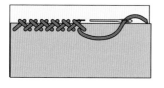

This stitch creates a row of overlapping diagonal stitches on the wrong side of the garment and then tiny invisible stitches on the right side of the garment. It is used to hem or secure a finished edge. With the needle facing to the left, catch a few threads of the main fabric from the wrong side of the garment, move about ½″ (12mm) to the right and catch a few threads from the hem or finished edge. Repeat to finish.

Whipstitch

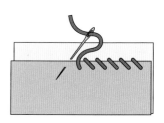

The whipstitch is a great stitch for hemming a chemise, doing the hand stitching for the waistband on bloomers or petticoats, or finishing the binding on a corset. It creates a nicely finished edge. Make slanted vertical stitches though the single layer of fabric, catching the fold of the hem, waistband, or binding.

Hand Embroidery

Hand embroidery is mostly decorative and can really vary from minimal detail to vast flower designs. If hand embroidery is something that brings you joy, I encourage you to take it as far as you would like. In corsetry, hand embroidery is also functional. Corset flossing is an embroidery technique invented by the Victorians to strengthen the ends of the boning channels where the boning could poke through. Embroidered eyelets also reinforce the corset grommet closure.

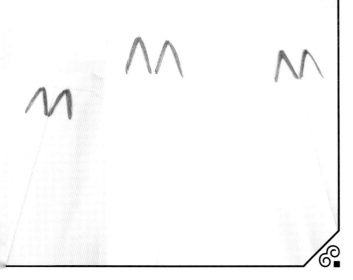

CORSET FLOSSING

There are dozens of forms of flossing on corsetry; it is like embroidery where anything you can imagine can probably be stitched in some form. The most straightforward form of flossing is stitching a V-shape at the top and bottom of the boning channel.

1. Using topstitching thread and an embroidery needle, thread the needle and knot the thread.

2. Starting at either the bottom or top of the boning channel, bring the needle from the back to the front of the corset where you want the point of the V to be.

3. Insert the needle 1″–3″ (2.5–7.6cm) down to the left in the channel stitching and through to the back of the corset, pulling the thread taut.

4. Bring the needle back to the front right next to the last stitch.

5. Go to the peak of the V and stitch through to the back.

6. Repeat with the stitches angled to the right. Continue stitching, alternating the direction, until the desired design is achieved.

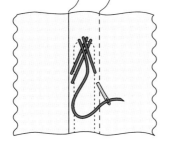

EMBROIDERED EYELETS

Embroidered eyelets are sewn over the edges of a hole in the fabric made by an awl. For corsets, grommets are a better choice than stitched eyelets. However, the embroidery will give the grommets extra strength as well as some decoration.

1. With topstitching thread and an embroidery needle, thread the needle and tie a knot.

2. Bury the knot in the back of the garment, close to the grommet.

3. Bring the needle through the grommet, around the edge, and through the fabric layers to the back.

4. Continue stitching around the grommet, pulling the thread taut.

5. When the entire grommet is encased in thread, tie off on the back with a tight knot.

Garment Fitting

Once we get to the construction portion of this book, measuring and fittings are going to be incredibly important. During every stage of costume making, fittings are important but they are extra important for the foundations. Since undergarments fit so close to the body, they determine how well you will be able to move as you add layers onto them. If your bodysuit rides too high or your corset is too tight, you could create uncomfortable issues for yourself down the line.

The best way to start every project is to measure yourself. Bodies change over time and it is important to measure often. If possible, have someone help you with your measurements to be sure they are accurate. I've created a guide to help you know where to measure.

1. BUST _____

2. WAIST _____

3. HIP _____

4. UPPER BUST _____

5. UPPER HIP _____

6. NECK _____

7. SHOULDER _____

8. ARM_____

9. WAIST _____

10. SHOULDER FRONT TO WAIST _____

11. SHOULDER BACK TO WAIST _____

12. WAIST TO KNEE_____

13. LEG INSEAM _____

14. WAIST TO ANKLE _____

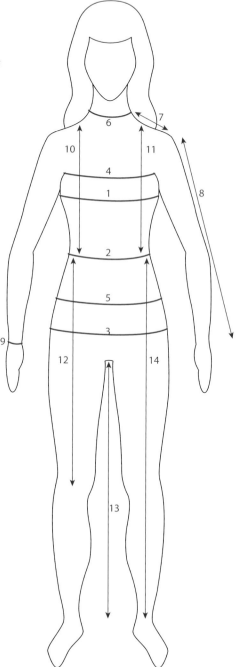

Body Measurement Chart

Another factor that comes into play with garment sewing is ease. Ease is the difference between the measurements of the finished garment and the measurement of your body. Ease is added into a garment so you can move around in it comfortably. A great way to figure out how you want your garment to fit is by making a mock-up first.

A mock-up is a test run. You make the garment out of a similar weight fabric, but not the actual fabric you plan to use. Mock-ups are typically made from muslin, but for stretchy garments like leggings, a cheap spandex is better. A garment made of spandex needs different ease than a garment made of muslin, so it is important to use the same type of fabric for the mock-up as the garment. Making a mock-up not only informs you on how the garment will fit but also acts as a test run for using a new pattern or technique.

To make the fitting adjustments easy, you can make the mock-up a size larger than your normal pattern size, then take in the mock-up as needed. For spandex garments, it is easier to add an extra ½″ (12mm) to all the seams and then take them in as needed.

When using a new pattern, make sure to shorten or lengthen it as necessary. Bodies are not only different in circumference but also in the length of torso and legs. While working on hoop skirts and petticoats, it's important to note that they can be a few inches short if you would like but if they are too long, you can trip on them or walk all over them.

I often fit my corset mock-ups over a T-shirt if I don't have a chemise made yet.

BALL GOWNS

Cosplay is such a creative art form and designing gowns and costumes is becoming the way of the future. When it comes to designing ball gowns, there is a rolodex of undergarments to choose from. The struggle will be creating the perfect undergarment combinations to fully execute the cosplay of your dreams.

Learning from historical costuming and sewing can really help inform construction techniques and final garment shapes, making it easier to create many costumes that we see on the silver screen as well as on convention floors.

This chapter is grouped into five segments covering corsets, hoop skirts, petticoats, chemises, and bloomers. Each chapter includes a brief history lesson on the garments as they changed throughout time, as well as a complete project so you can make your very own set of modern undergarments. While white is the most common fabric color of choice for many of these projects, I empower you to make your undergarments in whatever colors suit you or your project. Once you have learned the basics of constructing strong, long-lasting undergarments, you will be ready to add any embellishments your heart desires. I add ruffles and detailed stitches to anything and everything, and I love to play with color in my undergarments; it makes them more fun to create.

Ball Gown History

The Middle Ages were a time of glorious shapelessness, however following the Middle Ages and moving into the Renaissance, gowns and fashion moved toward a silhouette that required more than just an under tunic. There was more shape in garments; everything from sleeves to skirts started to change and take new shape. In the early 1500s, women's fashion started to take a more conical shape while men's fashion started to take a square shape emphasizing broad shoulders. During this time, the first version of the corset as well as the initial version of the hoop skirt, along with padding, appeared. The chemise, or shift, was still a very prominent garment during this time especially with the weather conditions in Western Europe and was always worn under a corset to protect the skin. As time went on, the hoop, corset, and chemise combo transformed dozens of times up to the twentieth century where hoop structures become less fashionable and eventually the corset and chemise were replaced by shapewear and slips.

COSPLAYER:
Casey Renee Cosplay

COSTUME: Ariel from
The Little Mermaid

*Photography by
Alexandra Lee Studios*

Anatomy of a Gowned Costume

Several garments work together to help create the silhouette of a gowned costume. We'll start with the garment worn closest to the skin. This is the *chemise*, or shift or smock, as it has been called throughout time. This garment has been around the longest of all the ones we will be making in this book. The purpose of the chemise in this context is to protect the wearer from the corset. But also, to protect the corset from the wearer.

Corset, bloomers, and hoop skirt

Photography by Alexandra Lee Studios

Corset, bloomers, hoop
skirt, and petticoat

The corset is a fitted garment starting at the chest and ending at or sometimes below the hip that helps create a specific shape through the torso. The size and shape of corsets have changed numerous times over the years, but the function of a corset has always been the same, and that is to shape the body of the wearer to the desired silhouette of the time. In the context of ball gowns, the corset is going to act as a replacement for the bra as well as a device to smooth out the midsection to create a definition between bust, waist, and hip.

The next layer is the **BLOOMERS**. These were worn for cleanliness. In modern costuming, we wear them for modesty as well. In both historical and contemporary fashion, we see bloomers with all kinds of frills.

The next thing to add, after the base layers, is the **HOOP SKIRT**. This garment has a very long history and has changed time and time again to fit the silhouette of the era. The primary purpose of the hoop skirt is to hold the shape of the dress or skirt that is worn over it.

Finally, we have the **PETTICOAT**. This is a many-layered garment that helps create the shape of the dress worn over it. It creates a barrier between the hoop and the outer skirt so boning doesn't poke through the fashion fabric. The petticoat can also be worn on its own, without a hoop, to provide fullness and pouf.

Chemise: The Most Important Undergarment

The chemise has been around since before Medieval times. Also known as the shift or smock, the chemise is quite possibly the essential foundation garment in this book. Throughout time, the chemise was treated like we treat modern underwear. People owned a few chemises, and they were the garment that absorbed sweat and kept the outer clothes clean. The chemise also protected the body from the corset. Men also wore a chemise with their trousers and often covered the chemise with doublets or robes.

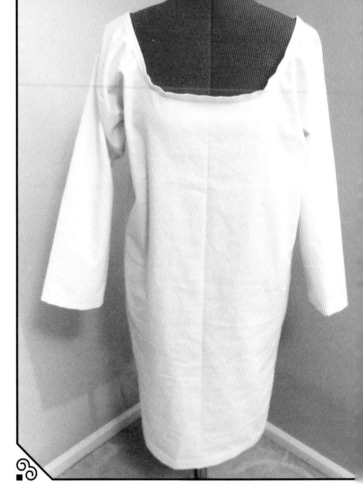

Historically, the chemise was made of rectangles and triangles cut from a piece of cloth to leave no waste. They were most often made of lightweight linen for the wicking properties in the linen. These garments were also slept in, and sometimes they featured embroidered detailing called "black work" on the collar and cuffs. Sleeve length also varied throughout time, starting as long sleeves and becoming three-quarter length sleeves in the 1500s. In the Victorian Era, chemises were sleeveless.

In the 1780s, the chemise had a fashion moment thanks to Marie Antoinette with the *Chemise a la Reine*. This garment was incredibly light and simple and consisted of layers of thin muslin. The layers typically were loosely draped around the body and belted around the waist. These garments made great lounging in the garden outfits.

A modern version of the chemise is closer to the slip or the cotton shirt. Slips today are often made of polyester-blend fabrics which don't allow for very much breathing. A chemise with a lace or bias tape strap would make a fantastic undergarment for gowns that need hidden straps to suit the bodice shape.

MAKE A CHEMISE

Finished size: Sized to the wearer

Materials

- 2–4 yards (1.8–3.7m) of linen, cotton lawn, or cotton broadcloth
- 1–2 yards (0.9–1.8m) of ½″ (12mm)-wide elastic
- 1–1½ yards (0.9–1.4m) of ½″ (12mm)-wide lace for straps
- 1–2 yards (0.9–1.9m) of additional fabric for ruffle (*optional*)
- 3–5 yards (2.8–4.6m) of lace for hem (*optional*)
- Fabric marking pen or tailor's chalk
- Rolled hem presser foot (*optional*)

Pattern Prep and Cutting

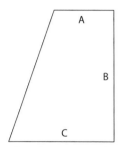

Draw a paper pattern following the instructions or draw the pattern directly on the fabric with a fabric marking pen or tailor's chalk.

Chemise pattern shape

FRONT/BACK

A. Refer to the Body Measurement Chart (page 36). Divide your bust measurement by 4, and then add 3″ (7.6cm). (Example: 34″ ÷ 4 = 8.5″ + 3″ = 11.5″.) Draw horizontal line A.

B. Measure from a point 4″ (10cm) above the bust to the knee or to mid-thigh if adding the optional ruffle. Draw a vertical line (B) from the right corner of line A straight down.

C. Multiply the A measurement by 1.5 and draw a horizontal line (C) from the bottom of line B toward the left to create line C. Join the left ends of line A and line C with a diagonal line.

Cut 2 pieces based on your measurements and the illustration, with line B positioned on the fabric fold.

RUFFLE

If you choose to add a hemline ruffle, multiply the C measurement by 4, then multiply by 2.5 for the total length. Cut pieces to equal the total by 5″ (12.7cm).

LACE

Measure over the shoulder from front to back at the upper bust. Add 1″ (2.5cm) for seam allowance at the ends. Cut 2 pieces of lace for the straps.

Optional: Multiply the C measurement by 4. Cut 1 piece of lace for the bottom of the chemise.

ELASTIC

Measure the upper bust 4″ (10.2cm) above the bust and add ½″ (12mm). Cut 1 piece.

Make It

Front/Back

1. Sew the front and back pieces together using French seams (page 32). *fig A*

2. Fold the top edge ¼″ (6mm) toward the wrong side and press.

3. Fold the folded edge ¾″ (19mm) toward the wrong side and press.

4. Sew next to the folded edge, leaving a 2″ (5.1cm) opening in the back.

5. Feed the elastic through the casing with a safety pin.

6. Making sure the elastic isn't twisted, overlap the ends of the elastic ½″ (12mm) and sew them together. *fig B*

7. Finish sewing the opening.

8. Try on the chemise and pin the lace straps to the front and back so the chemise fits comfortably. Machine stitch in place.

9. Make a folded hem (page 33), with the first fold ½″ (12mm) and the second fold 1″ 2.5cm).

10. Add lace to the hem by machine stitching in place (optional). *fig C*

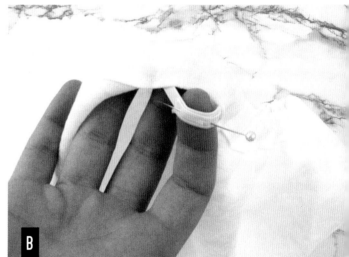

Ruffles (Optional)

1. Join the ruffle pieces end to end using a French seam (page 32).

2. Overcast stitch the top edge of the ruffle (page 32).

3. Hem the ruffle piece with a tiny rolled hem (page 33). *fig D*

4. Overedge stitch the bottom edge of the chemise.

5. Gather the ruffle using your preferred method (page 29).

6. Attach the ruffle to the chemise with right sides together, adjusting the gathering stitches as needed. *fig E*

7. If desired, sew lace to the chemise close to the ruffle seam. *fig F*

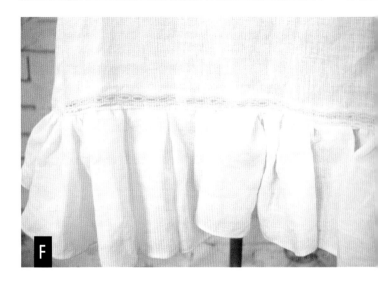

Corsets

Corsets Versus Stays

The earliest form of the corset as an undergarment is dated back to the 1500s and was called a pair of "bodies." At this time, the purpose of this garment was to create a rigid flatness in the bodice front with the curve of the breast peeking out over the top of the corset.

In the sixteenth and seventeenth centuries, "bodies" could be worn as both undergarments and outer garments. At this time, whalebone was frequently used in the creation of these undergarments with a busk made of wood, whalebone, or steel inserted at the front. These early corsets also had straps that went over the shoulder and sometimes had eyelets in them for detachable sleeves.

COSPLAYER: Casey Renee Cosplay
COSTUME: Rococo undergarments, original design

Photography by Alexandra Lee Studios

The inverted conical shape was the most common silhouette of the eighteenth century. The garment that helped create this shape was referred to as "stays," although that term can also mean the boning in the stay. The word "stays" came from the French word *estayer*, meaning to support. The V shape torso of this era was created from the way the stays pulled the shoulders down and back, while raising and lifting the breasts and ultimately improving the posture of the wearer by forcing them to sit up straighter. For more informal situations, "jumps" would have been worn. These were a quilted variety of stays that were made of linen and often embroidered.

Near the end of the eighteenth century, "short stays" become popular. These did not fall much further than right below the breast and allowed for a natural waist to the silhouette. These short stays were a very early precursor to the bra.

In the early Victorian era, the 1830s, the longer corset returned to support the breasts and narrow the waist. This was when the term corset was first used for this garment. At this time, steel was being used for boning and the shoulders became less of a prominent feature and the cinched waist started becoming popular. This is the famous corset silhouette many visualize today when they think about the corset.

Picking the Right Corset for Your Costume

Choosing a corset that suits your costume is a rather big task but it gets easier as you make more costumes. If you are making a historical costume from the 1780s, then doing research on stays during that decade is your first step. Researching how historians believed the garment was made, using patterns taken from extant garments, and even using authentic materials from the area can help make the actual corset-making process easier.

However, if we're talking about making corsets for fantastical characters out of a Disney movie, then we have a different set of problems that might need to be solved. In this case, I suggest two options; if it is a live-action version of something like Cinderella, you can research how the costume designer and makers developed the corset made for the film. Using images and behind-the-scenes videos, you can capture all sides of the garment and how it moves and try to replicate it.

The second option, which is my personal choice, is to use the costume designer's choice and historical references to help choose a corset shape that will work best for you and your project.

There are so many non-historical corsets that it can be hard to pick the right one for your project.

Start with the cut of the dress that will be worn over the corset. Is it strapless? Does it have a deep V-neck? Is it sheer? All of these dress features will modify the shape of the top of the corset. If the dress has a deep V-neck, consider making an under bust corset and wearing it

Under bust corset for a future project

with a bra. For one costume, I developed a corset that sits very low on my chest and back so that it would not be seen under the sheer fabric of the neck and back.

The length of the corset is determined by the type of skirt. If you are planning on a hoop, the corset often stops closer to the waist. In a dress like the one I made for a Morticia Addams costume, I chose to make a longer corset to smooth out my waist going into my hips and thus allowing me to create an illusion that my waist was much smaller than it is.

Corsetry Myths

There are several tropes or myths revolving around corsetry, and for your safety and the safety of anyone who happens to make and wear a corset, we should debunk some of these myths. Let's start with the belief that everyone had a desired 20″ (51cm) waist in a corset. Dress historians have been collecting data for quite some time now on the measurements of garments in the Victorian Era, and their data from over 800 garments show that corsets at the time were 27″ (69cm) and larger. While yes, there are those very few corsets that were under that, but it was not the norm.

To dive even deeper into the tiny waist topic, padding of the hip and bust in corsets, hoop skirts, panniers, and even sleeves could create the illusion of a smaller waist. All these techniques were used often.

A common myth is that people fainted from wearing corsets. While there probably were occasions when a corset wearer fainted due to heat exhaustion, this was far less likely happen if the corset was worn properly. There was a small group of people for a time practicing "tight-lacing," but for the most part, if you feel like you are going to faint in your corset, it is because the corset is the wrong size or it is laced too tight.

COSPLAYER: Casey Renee Cosplay
COSTUME: Morticia Addams from *The Addams Family*
Photography by Alexandra Lee Studios

Finally, there is a widespread misconception that you can't move or sit in a corset. There have been several corset challenges on Instagram of costume makers doing aerobics, push-ups, and even long-distance running in corsets to bust this myth. If you have made a properly-fitted corset and you are not lacing it too tight, you should have almost no added mobility issues. When I wear my corset, if I overeat food, I will feel some discomfort which is why I won't go to the Indian buffet in my corset.

COSPLAYER: Casey Renee Cosplay
COSTUME: Ariel from *The Little Mermaid*
Photography by Alexandra Lee Studios

MAKE A CORSET

When you lengthen or shorten the panels as indicated on the pattern, keep in mind that the length should be compatible with the available sizes of busks. If a busk is too short, the top and bottom edges of the corset will not be properly supported and will fold in or out and cause discomfort.

Before cutting into expensive fashion fabric and coutil, I highly recommend making a mock-up from less costly fabrics to ensure fit. To do this, cut the pattern pieces from a heavy canvas or even non-stretch denim. Sew each panel together according to the directions given here, and add boning and grommets. Instead of installing the busk, just sew the center front panels together. Then try on the corset over either a tank top, T-shirt, or shift. You should be able to breathe and expand your rib cage while still leaving 1″–2″ (2.5cm–5cm) opening at the back of the corset.

Materials

- 1 yard (9.1m) of cotton for lining
- 1 yard (9.1m) of coutil
- 1 yard (9.1m) of fashion fabric
- 7 yards (6.5m) of ¼″ (6mm)-wide boning
- Busk
- 3–4 yards (2.8–4.6m) of ½″ (12mm)-wide double-fold bias tape
- 20 or 22 sets of ⅜″ (10mm) grommets
- Grommet tool kit
- Awl
- 8 yards (7.4m) of corset lacing
- Topstitch thread (optional)

Pattern Prep and Cutting

A full-size download of the corset pattern is available; see Downloadable Patterns (page 30) for the link.

COTTON LINING AND COUTIL

Cut 2 each of Center Front, Side Front, Side, Side Back, and Back panels from both lining and coutil.

FASHION FABRIC

Cut 2 each of the above panels by pinning the cut coutil pieces to the wrong side of the fashion fabric, for a total of 10 panels (5 and 5 mirror image), and cutting the fashion fabric pieces approximately 1″ (2.5cm) larger all around than the coutil pieces.

COSPLAYER: Casey Renee Cosplay
COSTUME: Belle from *Beauty and the Beast*
Photography by Alexandra Lee Studios

Make It

Seam allowances are ⅝″ (16mm) unless otherwise noted.

Prepare the Fashion Fabric

1. Baste the coutil pieces to the fashion fabric pieces about ¼″ (6mm) away from the edges.

2. Press all the pieces, then trim the fashion fabric to match the coutil. Treat these pieces as one layer as you make the corset. *fig A*

Make the Fashion Fabric Layer

1. Arrange the basted and trimmed pieces into the right and left halves of the corset. Work with one half of the corset at a time. With the fashion fabric layers together, pin the side front piece to the center front piece starting at the notch and working to the ends. Note: In these examples, the fashion fabric is a white silk taffeta. *fig B*

2. Stitch the seam.

3. Press the seam open. Use a tailor's pressing ham to help with the curves.

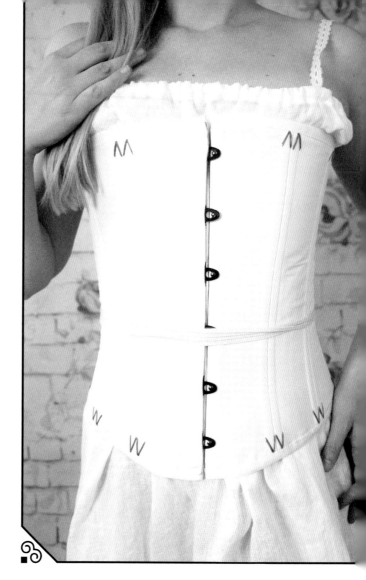

A

B

C

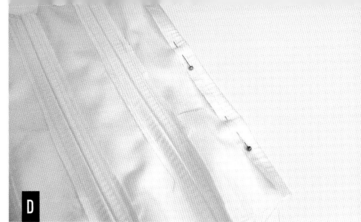

D

4. Stitch ⅜″ (10mm) from the seam on each side, catching the seam allowance in the stitching, to create the boning channels. *fig C*

5. Repeat this process to add the side, side back, and center back pieces.

6. Fold the straight edge of the center back panel ⅝″ (16mm) to the wrong side and stitch ⅜″ (10mm) away from the fold to create the center back boning channel. *fig D*

Make the Lining Layer

1. Make the lining layer the same as the fashion layer, but do not stitch the boning channels since the lining layer does not need them. *fig E*

E

Prepare and Add the Boning

1. Cut a piece of boning for each channel. Each piece should be ⅝″ (16mm) shorter than the boning channel on both the top and bottom edges. This leaves room for binding later. *fig F*

2. Clean the edges of the boning by clipping the corners of each edge at a 45° angle. Use a sanding stick or nail file to sand the edges to create a nice curve. *fig G*

3. Slide the boning pieces into the corresponding channel.

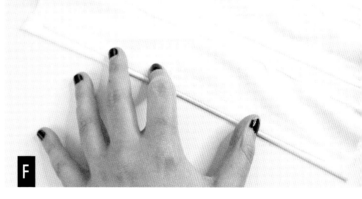

F

G

Busk Installation

At this point, there are right and left halves of the fashion fabric layer and of the lining layer.

BUSK LOOP HALF

1. Working with the right half of the corset, place the fashion fabric layer and lining layer right sides together, aligning the center front edges.

2. Place the busk right half (the side with the loops) on top of the lining ½˝ (12mm) away from the front, top, and bottom edges.

3. Mark the stitching line on the lining only between the loops. (There will be gaps in the seam to leave openings for the loops.) *fig H*

4. Pin the lining to the fashion fabric.

5. Sew on the lines marked, leaving gaps for the busk loops. Make sure to backstitch at the beginning and end of each stitching line. *fig I*

6. Press the seam open.

7. Position the busk half, with the loops through the gaps in the seam. *fig J*

8. Fold the fashion fabric and lining layers wrong sides together to encase the busk half.

9. Pin as close to the busk piece as possible. *fig K*

10. Sew along this edge using a zipper foot to get as close to the busk as possible without hitting the metal with the needle.

TIP *Warning! Sew this seam with precaution; if the needle hits the metal, it can shatter the needle.*

H

I

J

K

BUSK POST HALF

1. Working with the left half of the corset, place the fashion fabric layer and lining layer right sides together, aligning the center front edges and pin.

2. Sew the center front edges together ½″ (12mm) from the straight edge.

3. Fold the layers wrong sides together and press.

4. Line up the corset left half with the already finished right half.

5. On the fashion fabric layer, mark inside each loop for the post placement. *fig L*

6. Use an awl to pierce just the fashion fabric at each marking. *fig M*

7. Place the busk left half between the fashion fabric and the lining layers with the posts fitting in the holes.

8. Pin the layers together close to the busk. *fig N*

9. Sew along this edge using a zipper foot to get as close to the busk as possible without hitting the metal with the needle.

Attach the Layers

1. For each of the corset halves, pin the fashion fabric layer to the lining layer with wrong sides together. (Installing the busk should have aligned the layers.) Line up the seams and place as many pins as needed on both the top and the bottom edges.

2. Pin the center back as close to the back boning channel as possible. *fig O*

3. Using a zipper foot, sew ¼″ (6mm) away from the top and bottom edges. For the center back edges, sew as close to the back boning channel as possible.

I used weights to hold the corset flat while marking.

L

M

N

O

P

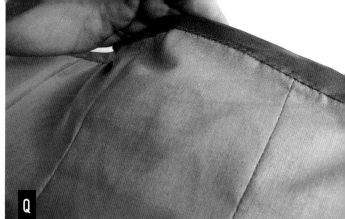

Q

Binding

1. Unfold the bias tape and pin the first fold to the fashion fabric side of the corset. Extend the tape 1″ (2.5cm) beyond the center front and center back edges. Fold the tape to the lining layer at the edges. *fig P*

2. Sew the bias tape to the corset, being careful not to hit the boning. Be sure to sew the folded ends of the bias tape at the center front and center back edges.

3. Fold the bias tape in half over the corset edge with the last fold and the ends tucked under and pin.

4. Sew the edge of the bias tape. This can be sewn by machine, but I prefer to whipstitch it on the inside. *fig Q*

5. Repeat for the other half of the corset.

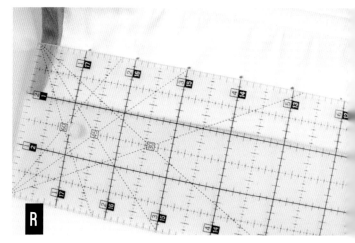

R

Grommets

1. Mark the grommet placement at the center back edge of each half of the corset, ½″ (12mm) away from the boning. Start from the top and mark every 1″ (2.5cm) down the corset back. The number of grommets will vary depending on torso length. *fig R*

2. Pierce through all the layers, using an awl the size of the grommet opening. *fig S*

S

3. Place the outer grommet piece (the half with the longer barrel) on the outside of the corset and the flat ring grommet piece on the inside.

4. Using the grommet kit tools, follow the manufacturer's directions to install the grommets. *fig T*

T

Optional Decorative Touches

Adding hand-embroidered eyelets and corset flossing are the final touch. These can be both functional and decorative. See Hand Stitches (page 35). *fig* U

Lacing your Corset

1. Starting at the top, thread the corset lacing from the inside to the outside of the corset. Cross over to the opposite side of the corset, and again thread from the inside to the outside. *fig* V

2. Stop threading at the waist. On both sides of the corset, thread the next grommet directly below the previous grommet, starting from the outside and going to the inside. (The example has 10 grommets, so this is from the fifth grommet to the sixth.) This vertical lacing becomes the loops or "bunny ears" that are pulled to tighten the corset. *fig* W

3. Continue to thread through the grommets back and forth until the last grommet. Tie the ends of the lacing together. Distribute the extra lacing to the bunny ears. When the corset is tightened, tie these lacing loops into a knot or double bow. *fig* X

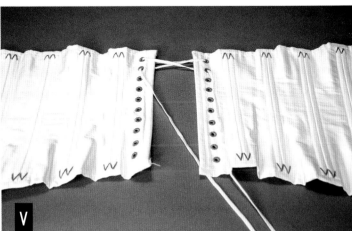

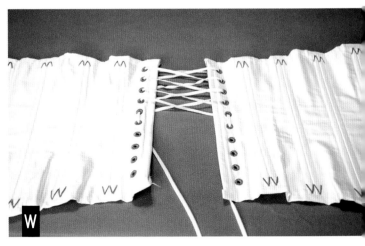

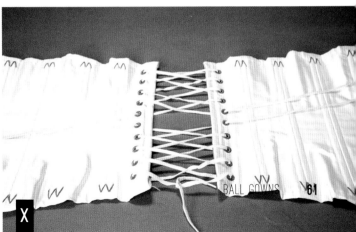

Bloomers

Bloomers originated from a garment called split drawers. Split drawers originated in the early to mid-nineteenth century and were a pant-like garment with an unsewn crotch seam and worn under gowns. They were lightweight and easy to move in, and made personal hygiene easier to manage with voluminous skirts and petticoats. Eventually, the split in the drawers went away, and they turned into the bloomers that we recognize today. Bloomers were worn by many women; those who liked to partake in sports and other activity found the bloomers allowed them movement while keeping them modest. Eventually, bloomers became a symbol for the suffragette movement, showing women in pant-like garments smashing the patriarchy.

In the late 1800s, the chemise and split drawers formed what was known as combinations. This was a romper-style garment that had the properties of a chemise on the top and the legs of the split drawers. The sleeveless chemise-like top gave the wearer protection from the corset, while the drawers on the bottom allowed for modesty underneath their dresses. These garments were often very frilly and filled with tucks, insertion lace, and even ruffled lace. They are genuinely some of the most beautiful undergarments throughout time and managed to prove that beauty can have a relationship with function in women's clothing.

In cosplay, bloomers are often worn under ball gowns of Disney princesses. They again act as a means of modesty, but they are also quite comfy and honestly could double as pajamas. They have been made in various lengths, from ending at the ankle to ending somewhere mid-thigh. Bloomer-type pants or even combinations can be worn in steampunk fashion paired with a corset and an aviator jacket for a more aesthetic look. Baby doll-style fashion also include bloomers with ruffles and frills for a more realized look. The best part about bloomers is they are relatively easy to make and can be modified in so many ways to create a pair uniquely for you.

MAKE BLOOMERS

Finished size: Sized to the wearer

Materials

- 2½–3 yards (2.3–1.9m) of cotton or linen
- 2–3 yards (1.4–1.9m) of 1″ (2.5cm)-wide twill tape or ribbon
- 1–2 yards (91cm–1.9m) of ¼″ (7mm)-wide elastic
- 1–2 yards (91cm–1.9m) of 1″ (2.5cm)-wide elastic
- 2–3 yards (1.9–2.8m) of ¼″–1″ (6–25mm)-wide lace (optional)
- Fabric marking pen or tailor's chalk

Pattern Prep and Cutting

A full-size download of the bloomer pattern is available; see Downloadable Patterns (page 30) for the link.

COTTON OR LINEN

Cut 2 bloomer pieces. Transfer the markings for the twill tape or ribbon to the wrong side of each piece.

TWILL TAPE/RIBBON AND ELASTIC

Measure the marking for the twill tape or ribbon on the pattern. Cut 2 lengths of twill tape or ribbon to the measurement.

Measure your calf and add ½″ (12mm). Cut 2 lengths of the ¼″ (6mm) wide elastic to the measurement.

Measure your waist and add ½″ (12mm). Cut 2 lengths of the 1″ (2.5cm) wide elastic to the measurement.

LACE (OPTIONAL)

Measure the leg opening of the pattern. Cut 2 lengths of lace to this measurement.

A

B

C

Make It

Legs

1. Hem the bottom edges of each piece with a folded hem (page 33).

2. If you choose to add the lace, machine stitch it to the bottom edges. *fig A*

3. Pin the twill tape or ribbon along the markings on the wrong side of the fabric for each piece. Stitch it in place along each edge, as shown. *fig B*

4. Feed the narrow elastic through the casing with a safety pin. Pin the end of the elastic to the beginning edge of the casing, then continue threading the elastic to the other edge. *fig C*

5. Remove the safety pin and pin the other end of the elastic to the casing edge. Sew the ends of the elastic to the fabric edges.

6. Sew the leg seams together on each piece using a French seam (page 32). *figs D & E*

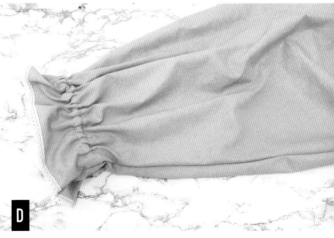

D

E

Waist

1. Turn one leg wrong side out and slide it inside the other leg, lining up the seams and the waist edges and pin.

2. Sew the crotch seam using a French seam (page 32). *fig F*

3. Fold the waist edge ½″ (12mm) to the wrong side and press.

4. Fold the pressed edge 1½″ (3.8cm) to the wrong side and press.

5. Sew next to the fold, leaving a 2″ (5.1cm) opening at the back. *fig G*

6. Feed the 1″ (2.5cm) wide elastic through the waist casing with a safety pin. Overlap the elastic ends ½″ (12mm) and sew the ends together.

7. Sew the opening closed.

Hoop Skirts

Hoop skirts are a wired structure that creates a floating affect when worn, most typically, under ball gowns. Without this wired structure, gowns would lay rather flat and a lose a lot of the drama their shaped silhouettes create.

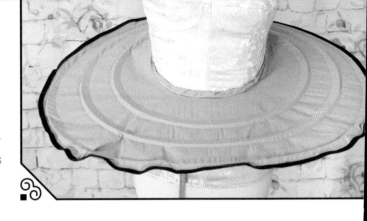

500 *Years of Hoops*

The Spanish farthingale first appeared as a hooped structure for women's garments in the late fifteenth and early sixteenth centuries. It was triangular or conical in shape and closed at the center front with ties; in the early years it was worn as an outer garment. Nearly one hundred years later, the same garment was worn underneath petticoats and dresses as a structure to create the shape often seen in Tudor fashion.

In the late sixteenth century, the farthingale dramatically changed into the French Wheel Farthingale, which was typically paired with a large "bum roll" (a crescent-shaped padded roll) to present the silhouette we now relate to Queen Elizabeth I. However, Spain was still very proud of their fashion endeavors, and they stuck with the Spanish farthingale making the shape more expansive and more glorious. These hoops were not only fashionable, but they were also a way for women to take up space and command attention.

COSPLAYER: Casey Renee Cosplay

COSTUME: Original design inspired by Sally Skellington from *The Nightmare Before Christmas*

Near the end of the seventeenth century, the hoop shape faded in popularity and disappeared until the mid-eighteenth century, when it developed into the pannier seen in Rococo fashion. The pannier spanned anywhere from 4 to 8 feet and was completely flat at the front and the back. The pannier grew smaller near the end of the century and eventually went away entirely by the century's turn.

In the late 1840s, a type of hoop made of horsehair and whalebone started to become popular, and by the 1850s, the cage crinoline was in full bloom with spring hoops. The cage crinoline transformed into the elliptical cage crinoline in the 1860s, which turned the hoop back into an elliptical shape.

From there, the hoop transformed into the bustle structure of the bustle era. The bustle structure changed quite a few times and offered a variety of sizes and shapes. A few of the different bustle understructures include the hooped bustle, imperial bustle, and the grand bustle petticoat combo. Towards the turn of the nineteenth century, hooped structures disappeared from fashion and, for the most part, only appeared for weddings, film, stage, and gala events.

Victorian corset and bustle structure

Photography by Alexandra Lee Studios

MAKE A HOOP SKIRT

Finished size: Sized to the wearer

Materials

- ⅛–¼ yard (11.4–22.9m) of cotton fabric
- ¼–½ yard (22.9–45.7m) of 20″ (50.8cm)-wide fusible interfacing
- 1 button ⅝″–1″ (1.6cm–2.5cm) diameter
- 22 yards (20.2m) of 1″ (2.5cm)-wide twill tape
- 45 yards (41.4m) of ½″ (12mm)-wide steel boning wire
- 45 yards (41.4m) of ¾″ (1.9cm)-wide bone casing
- Marking pen
- Plasti Dip coating
- Masking tape

Cutting

COTTON AND INTERFACING

Measure your waist and add 2″ (5cm). Cut 1 strip (or piece together more strips as necessary) to equal this measurement by 3″ (7.6cm) wide from both.

TIP *If the hoop will be worn with a corset, use the waist measurement from the corset.*

TWILL TAPE

Cut 9 strips of twill tape.

If you are 5′7″ (170cm) or shorter, cut the strips of twill tape 82″ (208cm) long.

If you are taller than 5′7″ (170cm), cut the strips of twill tape 87″ (221cm) long.

BONING WIRE AND BONE CASING

If you are 5′7″ (170cm) or shorter, omit the 13th hoop.

Cut 12 or 13 pieces of both boning wire and bone casing into the following lengths:

55″, 71″, 85″, 96″, 108″, 118″, 128″, 134″, 140″, 146″, 150″, 154″, 157″ (140cm, 180cm, 216cm, 244cm, 274cm, 300cm, 325cm, 340cm, 356cm, 371cm, 381cm, 391cm, 399cm)

Number them 1 (smallest) through 12 or 13 (largest).

Make It

Make the Waistband

1. Adhere the interfacing to the wrong side of the cotton strip, following the manufacturer's instructions.

2. Divide your waist measurement by 9 to determine the spacing for the twill tape.

3. Fold the waistband in half lengthwise and mark the center at the fold. Then make four markings to the left, each the distance apart you determined in the previous step. Repeat to the right. *figs A & B*

4. Fold and press the ends of the waistband ½˝ (12mm) to the wrong side.

5. Fold and press the long edges ½˝ (12mm) to the wrong side. Fold and press the waistband in half lengthwise with wrong sides together. *fig C*

6. Fold a length of twill tape in half. Insert the ends ½˝ (12mm) inside the folded waistband at the first marking. Pin the tape ends in place. Continue inserting the lengths of twill tape at the markings. Use clips to hold the waistband edges together between the lengths of twill tape. *fig D*

7. Sew the edges of the waistband together.

8. Place the waistband around your waist and mark the button and buttonhole placement. Make a buttonhole and sew the button in place. *fig E*

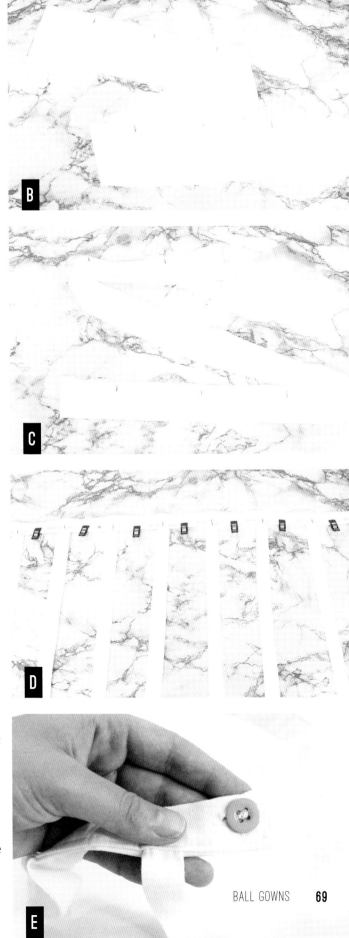

Mark the Twill Tape

Mark the placement for the hoops. Starting from the bottom fold and working up to the waistband, mark the following measurements onto the twill tape:

2½″, 5″, 7½″, 10¾″, 14″, 17¼″, 20½″, 23¾″, 27″, 30¼″, 33½″, 36¾″ (6.4cm, 12.7cm, 19.1cm, 27.3cm, 35.6cm, 43.8cm, 52.1cm, 60.3cm, 68.6cm, 76.8cm, 85.1cm, 93.3cm).

Prepare the Boning Wire

Dip both ends of the cut wire pieces into the Plasti Dip coating two to four times to coat the ends, following the manufacturer's instructions. Allow to dry for at least 4 hours before using the pieces. *fig F*

Assemble the Hoop

1. Mark the bone casing pieces so they will line up with the 9 lengths of twill tape. The measurements below are based on the cut lengths of the bone casing, minus 2″ (5.1cm), and divided by 9. The totals are rounded to the nearest ⅛ of an inch. Working from the smallest to the largest pieces of bone casing, mark these intervals:

5⅞″, 7⅝″, 9¼″, 10⅜″, 11¾″, 12⅞″, 14″, 14⅝″, 15⅜″, 16″, 16½″, 16⅞″, 17¼″ (14.9cm, 19.4cm, 23.5, 26.4cm, 29.8cm, 32.7cm, 35.6cm, 37.1cm, 39.1cm, 40.6cm, 41.9cm, 42.9cm, 43.8cm). *fig G*

2. Insert the boning wire into the corresponding marked pieces of bone casing.

3. Starting at the front center of the bottom hoop, feed the largest piece (for your height) of wired casing through the twill tape layers and pin. Work the wired casing through the remaining lengths of twill tape toward the center back. Pin the twill tape together at each intersection. As the wired casing is pinned to the lengths of twill tape, it curves and begins to form a circle and the shape of the hoop. *fig H*

4. Overlap the ends of the boning wire 2˝ (5.1cm) and secure with masking tape. Feed the overlap into the casing.

5. Sew the casing closed by hand. *fig I*

6. Hand sew the bone casing to the twill tape at each intersection.

7. Repeat for the remaining 11 or 12 hoops, working from the bottom to the top. *fig J*

Note: When you wear the hoop skirt, the opening can be in the front, back, or side. It's properly weighted so it can be worn in any direction necessary. When I get dressed by myself, the button is in the front; when I have help, it's typically in the back.

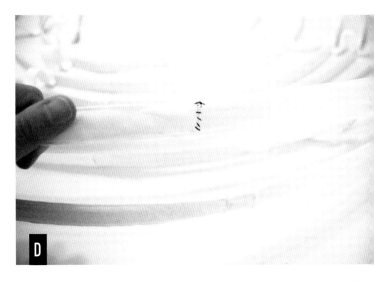

D

E

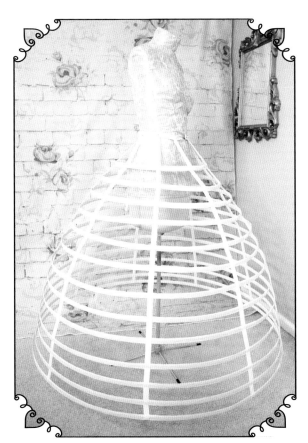

Petticoats

History, Size, and Shape

Like all the garments in the ball gown section of this book, the petticoat has had many face-lifts throughout the years. The origin of the petticoat dates to the fourteenth century and derives from the term *pety cote* meaning small coat. In the sixteenth century, the petticoat was most often a brocade underskirt that was seen between sections of the gown. It provided warmth and a bit of padding to make the gown appear fuller or larger than it was. The purpose of the petticoat has not changed since that time, and, as hooped understructures became popular, the goal of the petticoats has been to smooth out the shape of the overskirts so that the hoop would not be noticeable.

Throughout history, petticoats have been made of various materials, from brocade to linen, silk, and cotton organdy. Until the nineteenth century, petticoats were often a visible garment, and although they were often designed to help create structure, they could be very ornate. In the eighteenth century, quilted petticoats were popular. These were exactly like what they sound, layers of fabric sewn together to create a quilt, and then gathered down at the waist and worn under an overskirt or dress. The quilting on these petticoats was done by hand and often had hundreds of hours of intricate stitching to create beautiful flowers or bow details. Some petticoats of the era also had ruffles and frills and appeared to be just as fancy as the *robe a la francaise* they were paired with.

Layered petticoats started to appear in the eighteenth century and moving into the nineteenth century, layering became an integral part of gown structure. Before the cage crinoline, in the 1830s, several starched cotton organdy

petticoats were used to create the fullness of a skirt. Petticoats use a combination of tucks, cording, and flounces to create more space and give the skirts worn over them that extra oomph. Petticoats were (and are) often paired with hooped structures like the pannier, lobster tail bustle, and cage crinoline. These pairings changed the shape of the petticoat, sometimes dramatically. A petticoat worn over a pannier had an entirely different amount of fabric, decoration, and shape than one that fit over a lobster-tail bustle structure. Even a petticoat worn by itself in the 1890s had a wildly different shape than one meant for the 1840s.

COSPLAYER: Casey Renee Cosplay
COSTUME: Anne Boleyn
Photography by Alexandra Lee Studios

In the early 1900s the petticoat started to fizzle out as the silhouette changed into a slimmer, sleeker look. It wasn't until the 1950s that we started seeing them again; this time, they took the form of a petticoat that is more recognizable today in cosplay. With designers like Dior creating very fluffy skirt portions of gowns and emphasizing the tiny waist of the model, petticoats were back in business. The petticoat of the 1950s was a tiered petticoat, meaning that starting at the waist, the tier was smaller, and tiers were added that doubled or tripled in size to create a cake-like effect.

In cosplay, petticoats vary from super short, thigh-length petticoats with lots of layers and flounces to mermaid-style petticoats that are fitted until the knee and then are filled with layers of fabric from the knee down. Cosplayers create petticoats that are short in the front and long in the back. They pair them with hoops or just wear them on their own. What is magical about petticoats is that once you start to learn how the tiers, ruffles, and layers work together, you can mold them to fit the style that you want. Petticoats are still used in fashion today too; artists like Christian Siriano create entire lines of clothing inspired by these ruffled, tiered garments. Lolita fashion uses petticoats and bloomers in their aesthetic for both structure and added cuteness. Even vintage-inspired or reproduction fashion uses petticoats to duplicate the silhouettes of the 1950s and 1960s. Layered skirts are here to stay, and it will be fun to see how they might change in the future.

COSPLAYER: Casey Renee Cosplay
COSTUME: Alice from *Alice in Wonderland*
Photography by Alexandra Lee Studios

MAKE A PETTICOAT

Finished size: Sized to the wearer

This petticoat is made to fit over the hoop skirt and the lengths are based on the hoop skirt (page 68). It is best to review the petticoat size and fabric yardage charts (page 138) and determine how much fabric you need before buying the fabric. The petticoat has two layers: the inner layer is a cotton circle skirt with an organza flounce plus two organza tiers also with flounces. The outer layer is an organza circle skirt with a flounce.

Materials

- 6–8 yards (5.5–7.3 meters) of cotton
- 22–30 yards (20–27.9 meters) of organza
- ¼–½ yard (22.9–45.7m) of 20″ (50.9cm)-wide fusible interfacing
- 2 hook and eye sets
- 1 spool of 20lb fishing line
- Rolled hem presser foot
- Metallic thread (*optional*)
- Measuring tape
- Fabric marking pen

Cutting

Measure your waist and the length from your waist to the 10th hoop on the hoop skirt (page 68). Use these measurements to find the appropriate sizes listed on Charts 1–4 (see Appendix, pages 138–141). The charts are organized first by length, then by waist size.

COTTON

Circle Skirt

Refer to Chart 1 (page 138). Use your length and waist measurements to find your waist radius and hem radius sizes. Fold a piece of cotton that is at least twice the length of your hem radius in half crosswise. From the corner fold, measure and mark the waist radius (dotted line) and the hem radius (solid line). Repeat on another length of fabric to cut 2 circle skirt pieces. Each cut piece will form a half circle. *figs A & B*

Refold the pieces. From the waist radius, measure and mark the placement for the lower and upper tiers using Chart 2 (page 139) and Chart 3 (page 140) on both pieces.

Waistband

Measure your waist and add 3″ (7.6cm). Cut 1 strip (or piece together more strips as necessary) to equal this measurement by 3″ (7.6cm) wide.

INTERFACING

Cut 1 strip (or strips) the same size as the cotton waistband.

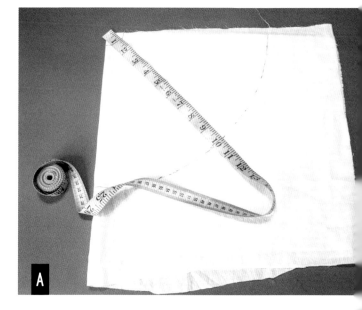

A

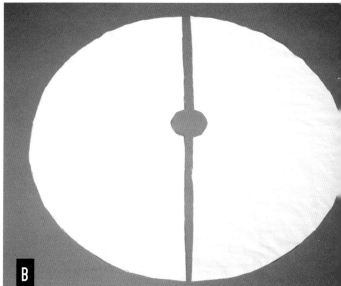

B

ORGANZA

Circle Skirt

Use your length and waist measurements to find your waist radius and hem radius sizes on Chart 4 (page 141). The hem radius is about 2″ (5.1cm) more than for the cotton circle skirt. Follow the steps for the cotton circle skirt to cut 2 circle skirt pieces.

Flounces

Cut all flounces 8″ (20.3cm) wide by the width of the fabric. Use your length and waist measurements to find the total length needed for the 4 flounces. Label the cut pieces with the number of the flounce. *fig C*

Flounce 1: Use Chart 1 (page 138) for the flounce length.

Flounce 2: Use Chart 2 (page 139) for the flounce length.

Flounce 3: Use Chart 3 (page 140) for the flounce length.

Flounce 4: Use Chart 4 (page 141) for the flounce length.

Tiers

Use your length and waist measurements to find the width (in the first column) and length to cut the tiers. Label the cut pieces with the name of the tier.

Lower Tier: Use Chart 2 (page 139) for the tier width and length.

Upper Tier: Use Chart 3 (page 140) for the tier width and length.

Note: The width of each tier is the measurement from the placement markings to the flounce; the length is the total amount of fabric that will be gathered and attached at the placement markings.

TIP *To make cutting the flounces easier, divide the length of the flounce by the width of the fabric to determine the number of pieces to cut. Round up to a whole number. Use the full width of the cut pieces even if the total is more than the listed lengths; the flounces will just have extra fullness.*

Make It

Make the Flounces

Keep the flounces labeled until you are ready to sew. Begin with Flounce 1 and follow the same steps for all four flounces.

1. Pin and sew together the selvage edges of all the flounce strips to make one continuous strip. Use a ½˝ (12cm) seam allowance. *fig A*

2. Attach the rolled hem presser foot and hem the bottom edge of the flounce using a zigzag stitch and including the fishing line (see Hems, page 33). Sew with metallic thread if you choose. *fig B*

3. Serge or zigzag stitch the top edge of the flounce to prevent raveling.

NOTE ◆ *If desired, serging the top edge can at the same time gather up the top edge of the flounce. This is done by adjusting the serger tension. In my experience, it doesn't ruffle it enough, so adjustments need to be made as you sew.*

4. To gather the fabric, use the preferred foot attachment (page 29) and sew gathering stitches no more than ⅝˝ (16mm) from the top edge. *fig C*

5. Set aside the gathered flounces.

Make the Tiers

1. Pin and sew together the edges of the Upper Tier strips to make one continuous strip. Use a ½˝ (12cm) seam allowance.

2. Serge or zigzag stitch the top and bottom edges of the tier to prevent raveling.

3. Gather the top edge as was done for the flounces.

4. Repeat for the Lower Tier.

Make the Circle Skirt Layers

1. With right sides together and using a ½˝ (12mm) seam allowance, sew the cotton circle skirt pieces together on one straight edge, as shown. *fig D*

2. Repeat with the other straight edge, leaving 10˝ (25.4cm) unsewn at the top.

3. Serge or zigzag the bottom edge.

4. Repeat with the organza circle skirt pieces.

Inner Layer Assembly

1. Sew the ruffled edge of Flounce 1 to the bottom of the cotton circle skirt. Adjust the gathers so the flounce fits the bottom edge of the skirt layer. *fig E*

2. Sew the ruffled edge of Flounce 2 to the bottom edge of the Lower Tier.

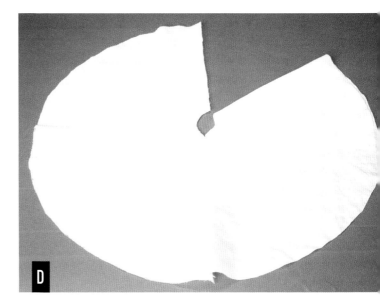

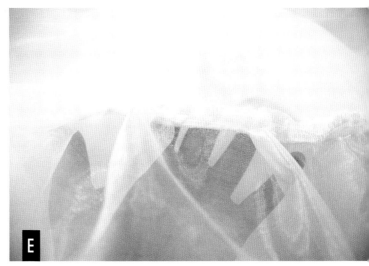

3. Pin and sew the *wrong* side of the Lower Tier to the *right* side of the cotton circle skirt along the placement markings. Adjust the gathers as needed. *fig F*

4. Sew the ruffled edge of Flounce 3 to the bottom edge of the Upper Tier.

5. Pin and sew the *wrong* side of the Upper Tier to the *right* side of the cotton circle skirt along the placement markings. Adjust the gathers as needed. *fig G*

F

G

Outer Layer Assembly

1. Sew the ruffled edge of Flounce 4 to the bottom edge of the organza circle skirt.

2. Sew the *wrong* side of the organza circle skirt to the *right* side of the cotton circle skirt at the waist. *fig H*

Make the Waistband and Finish the Petticoat

1. Fuse or sew the interfacing to the wrong side of the cotton waistband following the manufacturer's instructions.

2. Fold and press the short ends of the waistband ½" (12mm) to the wrong side.

3. Fold and press the waistband in half lengthwise.

4. Fold and press the long edges ½" (12mm) to the wrong side. *fig I*

5. Pin the waistband over the stitched waist edges to enclose the two layers of fabric.

6. Sew the edges of the waistband together next to the folds, as shown. *fig J*

7. Hand sew hooks and eyes on either side of the waistband opening. *fig K*

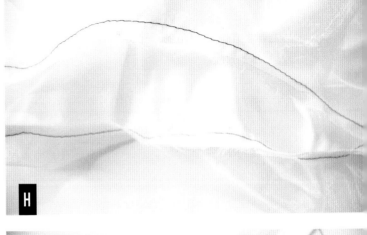

H

I

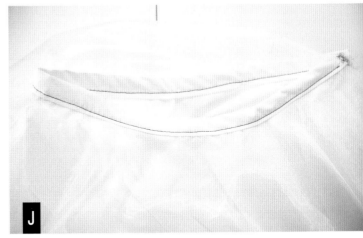

J

K

BODYSUITS FOR ARMOR AND ANIME

As costume designs in film and television become more challenging to reproduce, cosplayers must learn new skills and new combinations of skills to achieve screen accuracy. This means that adding some basic sewing skills to the long list of skills you already know will make your costuming adventures easier and more enjoyable. Being able to sew also allows for more customizations from sleeve length to the straps necessary to attach armor.

Armor is typically worn on top of another garment. Sometimes that garment is made of chain mail, sometimes it's a quilted gambeson, and other times, it might be something as simple as leggings or a bodysuit. While those garments are relatively easy to source and quite affordable, they do not always have the best fit. If they do not fit well, they could create issues with the fit of any armor attached to them later. Being able to sew a custom bodysuit allows for modifications to create a perfect character replica or to add your own flair to a design.

COSPLAYER: nyvednaproductions
COSTUME: Shuri from Black Panther
Photography by Alexandra Lee Studios

Sailor Fuku Fashion

A fuku or Sailor Fuku is the outfit worn by Sailor Scouts; it's also known as a Sailor costume. For those who are a fan of the Sailor Moon franchise, these costumes are probably very familiar to you. They are made of a base spandex suit that typically has snaps and attachments for the skirt, bows, and hip rolls for each character. Sailor Scouts have their own color scheme and slightly different design elements that make each of them unique. Many of these characters even get slight costume changes throughout the run of the show. These costumes are magical because as simple as they look to make, they can be incredibly detailed and meticulous in both fitting and design. The magical girl aesthetic has influenced a variety of "skins" in video games, mash-ups, and more. This same concept can even be applied to school-girl costumes.

The undergarments worn by Sailor Scout Fuku are important for modesty purposes but are also the final part of the costume. So, when you see Sailor Moon in all her blue and white glory, the white of the garment has many purposes. I've already mentioned modesty and the ability to attach the pieces to it as a base, but lastly, the fuku acts as the shirt and sleeves of the costume. These multipurpose garments teach us a lot about creating undergarments that also need to look as good as the pieces worn over them.

With a garment that has so much importance visually and structurally, it's crucial to make sure that it not only fits well but that it can hold up to the weight of everything being attached to it. This means that durable spandex is probably the best fabric choice, and it also means that seam placement and strength are very important. This same thought process can and should be applied to any kind of bodysuit meant to be worn under armor or even on its own.

COSPLAYER: LunarLyn
COSTUME: Sailor Moon Cosplay Progress

COSPLAYER: LunarLyn

COSTUME: Sailor Venus from *Sailor Moon* manga series

Photography by Deegan Marie Photography

Bodysuits

Benefits of the Bodysuit under Armor

The most significant benefit to having a bodysuit to wear under armor is comfort. Since armor can be made of various materials, having a layer of fabric to protect your skin can make wearing your costume easier. Spandex, from which most bodysuits are made, is also very easy to wash, and therefore it can be used to absorb sweat and body oils and allow the armor pieces to live a longer life.

As previously mentioned, bodysuits are often used to hold armor attachments. Attaching pieces to a base makes movement more fluid. The base layer allows for movement trials so changes can be made to ensure that the armor pieces don't rub against each other or the wearer. Ultimately, bodysuits allow the cosplayer to be as agile as humanly possible while wearing an armored costume. Creating a custom bodysuit can also be a great way to hide electrical cords and batteries.

Let's be honest here, the ultimate reason you would need to create a custom bodysuit is if the costume design had a bodysuit that was in some way unique or hard to find. Bodysuits with crazy amounts of panels and topstitching can be difficult to source, so making one is probably the only way to have one that suits all the needs of the costume. Learning how to create a basic bodysuit can also give you the base and tools for creating a bodysuit with fake muscles or a bodysuit that makes your skin look green or give you a whole body of tattoos. Not to mention custom character designs, like when you make your *World of Warcraft* character, and decide you needed a particular blue dragonscale suit under your armor. This kind of design can be frightening to tackle at first, but with the power of custom-printed fabric that you can design yourself, it's possible to sew any bodysuit to wear under the armor of your character. The first project in this chapter is the creation of personalized base bodysuit pattern for you to build and modify as many times as you would like.

COSPLAYER:
Nospaceship

COSTUME: Ronin Warriors from *Samurai Troopers* anime

Photography by Alexandra Lee Studios

COSPLAYER: GinozaCostuming

COSTUME: Death Knight from *World of Warcraft* video game

Photography by Alexandra Lee Studios

BUILD YOUR OWN BODYSUIT

You can use a made-to-fit bodysuit block or pattern to custom create any bodysuit you ever need. A block is a basic sewing pattern template that is custom made to fit your body, and from which you can create an infinite number of styles. For this project, you create a duct tape bodysuit to help you make your pattern, and then use that pattern to make a mock-up. Once you make the duct tape bodysuit, you cut it apart and trace the pieces (arm, leg, torso front and torso back) to create the patterns. Then use the pattern pieces to make a mock-up out of spandex. If the mock-up looks good, use the pattern pieces to make your project. If necessary, make fitting adjustments on the mock-up, until it fits to perfection. Be sure to transfer the fit adjustments to the pattern pieces, so you don't have to make the same fit adjustments every time you make a bodysuit. And use the pattern pieces over and over again to create design modifications.

NOTE ◆ *You need a friend to help you with this project, someone with whom you are very comfortable!*

Materials

- Plastic cling wrap
- Duct tape (not black)
- Permanent marker
- Pattern or craft paper
- Pattern weights
- French curve ruler
- Straight ruler
- Craft scissors
- Pattern or craft paper
- Zipper foot
- Safety pins
- Seam ripper
- 2–3 yards (1.9–2.8m) of inexpensive spandex
- 2–3 yards (1.9–2.8m) of fashion spandex
- 16″–22″ (41–56cm) zipper

This garment is simply a mock-up for the bodysuit instructions, so it's okay if the color of the fabric hurts your eyes slightly.

Make a Duct Tape Bodysuit

1. Wear a thin layer of clothes. Wrap the cling wrap around your torso from the top of your legs to your shoulders, but do not wrap your legs or shoulders yet.

2. Wrap only one arm. This will keep you more comfortable and allow you to move. Lift your arm and wrap the cling wrap around the shoulder, up to your neck, and under the arm, until your armpit is covered; you might have to trim the cling wrap in the gap between the arm and the body.

TIP *Use smaller strips of duct tape to secure the cling wrap while building the cling wrap base.*

3. Wrap the cling wrap from your shoulder to your wrist.

TIP *It's best if you wrap the cling wrap past the points on your body that you need for the pattern.*

4. Place strips of duct tape over the cling wrap to cover the torso; make sure not to pull the tape taut. Avoid stretching the tape as this makes creating the pattern difficult. Wrap the arm with duct tape.

5. To connect the leg to the torso, stand with your legs wide apart and wrap cling wrap around one leg from torso to ankle.

6. Cover the cling wrap with strips of duct tape.

NOTE ◆ *Don't lock the knee while taping.*

TIP *Precut lots of strips of duct tape and stick them on a nearby chair or table for quick access.*

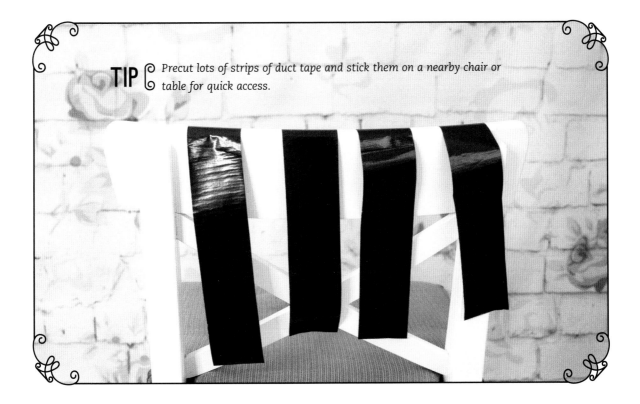

7. Use the marker to draw the following seamlines or fitting lines: the shoulder seam, neckline, center front, center back, side seams, the armhole (connecting it to the side seam), the seam that connects the leg to the body, and the leg inseam.

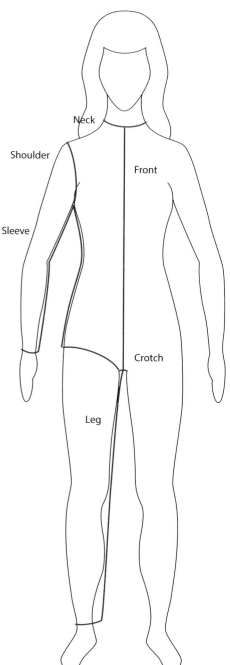

TIP *Mark notches with the pen at all the seamlines to help align pieces when sewing.*

8. To get out of the duct tape bodysuit, cut the torso on the side opposite of the marked seam lines and wrapped arm and leg.

9. Then, on the same side, cut from the shoulder to the neck.

TIP *When cutting the duct tape bodysuit open, make each snip small and thoughtful and go slow, so you don't cut into your clothes.*

10. Cut the underarm seam and around the shoulder to completely remove the arm piece.

11. Cut the leg inseam and across the crotch seam; this should enable you to get out of the bodysuit.

Prep the Pattern

1. Cut apart the duct tape pieces so that you have torso front, torso back, sleeve, and leg pieces. Cut on the center lines of the torso front and back pieces to yield half pattern pieces.

2. Label the pieces and add notches at this point if you didn't already mark them.

3. Use fabric weights to lay each piece as flat as possible. *fig A*

4. Trace each piece onto the paper, understanding that the sleeve and leg pieces should be straight on the sides and at the bottom. The shoulder seam should also be straight on the torso pieces.

5. Clean up the curves with a French curve ruler and the straight edges with a straight ruler. *fig B*

6. Add ½″ (12mm) seam allowances around every piece at the seamlines except on the center front, since this will be placed on a fabric fold. Feel free to write as much information as you need directly on the pattern pieces. It's a good idea to label the notches on the sleeve cap for the front (F), center or shoulder seam (C), and back (B). *fig C*

7. Label each piece and cut the paper pattern pieces. *fig D*

It's okay if your fabric weights are unconventional as long as they get the job done.

A

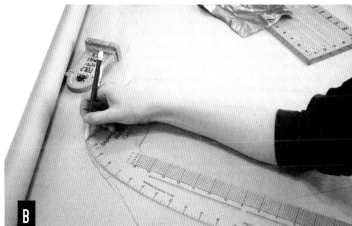

B

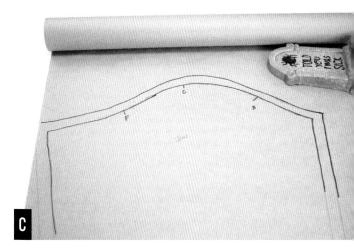

C

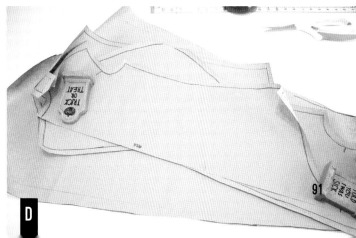

D

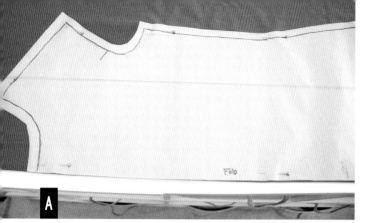

A

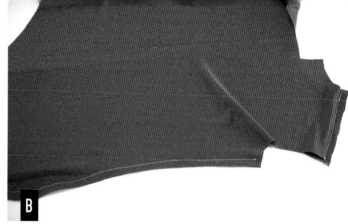

B

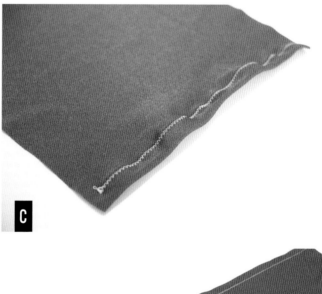

C

Make a Mock-up Bodysuit

Seam allowance is ½˝ (12mm) unless otherwise noted.

Use a stretch stitch (page 32).

1. Fold the practice fabric in half lengthwise.

2. Position the torso front pattern so the center front is along the fabric fold. Pin in place and cut 1 front piece. *fig A*

3. Cut 2 each using the torso back, sleeve, and leg pattern pieces.

4. With right sides together, use a stretch stitch to sew the torso front to the torso back at the side seams and at the shoulder seams. *fig B*

NOTE ◆ *For the mock-up, avoid sewing with a serger, or any machine that trims the seam allowance, in case you need to let the seams out.*

5. Fold the bottom edges of the sleeves and legs ½˝ (12mm) to the wrong side and sew the hems. *fig C*

6. With right sides together, sew the underarm sleeve seams. *fig D*

7. With right sides together, sew the leg inseams.

8. With right sides together, sew the sleeves to the torso, lining up the notches and the seams. *fig E*

D

E

9. Mark the length of the zipper on the torso back center edges, measuring from the neck down.

10. With right sides together, sew the torso back pieces together below the zipper marking. *fig F*

11. With right sides together, sew the crotch seam. Sew the leg pieces to the torso piece, lining up the notches and the seams.

12. Fold the neckline edges ½˝ (13mm) to the wrong side and sew.

13. Baste the open portion of the center back seam. *fig G*

13. Pin the zipper in place, following the instructions on the zipper package for a centered application. *fig H*

14. Install a zipper foot and sew the zipper tape in place.

15. Use a seam ripper to remove the basting stitches to reveal the zipper. *fig I*

16. Stitch across the bottom of the zipper. *fig J*

Fitting

1. Try the bodysuit on, look in the mirror, and note where it doesn't fit well. *figs A & B*

NOTE ◆ *It's extremely rare for a bodysuit to fit at this stage which is why it's important to make a mock-up.*

2. Turn the bodysuit inside out and put it back on. *fig C*

3. Use safety pins along the seams to take in the areas that are too big or need to be raised.

4. Ask your helper to place pins along the back seam as needed; safety pin the lower portion of the seam but for the zipper area, ask your friend to measure how much that seam needs to be taken in or let out and mark that adjustment.

TIP *To fit through the torso, it's best to pinch each side seam in at the same time to get the fit right.*

The areas of focus on my bodysuit were the too long and large torso area, the large leg area, and the need to raise the seams at the legs a bit higher.

5. For the leg seam at the torso, pull from whichever direction has more fabric and safety pin it together. *fig D*

6. Adjust the shoulder seam if the torso piece is too long after adjusting the leg seams.

7. For the arms, start at the armpit and safety pin that seam moving toward the wrist.

8. For the legs, start at the crotch and safety pin that seam moving toward to the ankle.

9. If you need to, rip out any seams or the zipper before sewing the adjustments.

10. True up the new sewing lines by marking along the safety pins with a marker.

11. Sew the new seams.

12. Fit to your body again and repeat until the bodysuit fits. Trim any extra seam allowance to ½˝ (12mm).

13. Take your bodysuit apart with a seam ripper and either make new paper pattern pieces or adjust your current ones with the modified mock-up piece. *fig E*

NOTE ◆ *At this point, you already know how to put your bodysuit pattern together. If you didn't need to make fit adjustments and then take the mock-up apart to note the changes on the pattern pieces; you can keep it as your bodysuit for your costume, or you could make a new one with higher quality materials.*

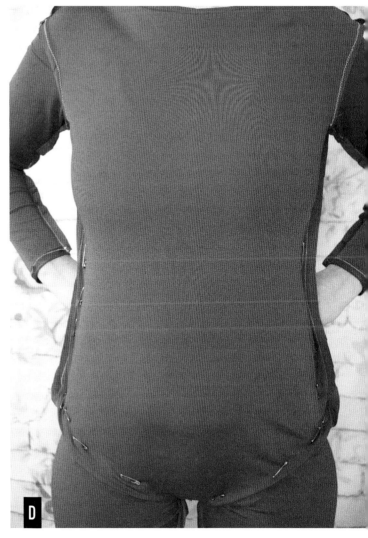

Bodysuit Customizations

Now that you have your own custom bodysuit pattern it's easy to customize it in order to make the costume of your dreams. It's easy to readjust the zipper, redraw the neckline, and even add or remove sleeves.

Front Zipper

1. Refer to your pattern pieces and cut 1 torso back on the fabric fold, eliminating the seam allowance.

2. Add ½˝ (12mm) seam allowance to the center front of the torso front and cut 2 fabric pieces, instead of placing the piece on the fabric fold.

3. Baste the center front seam and insert the zipper, following the instructions on the zipper packaging for a centered application.

Front Zipper with Collar

You'll need ¼ yard (22.9m) of spandex. Use ½˝ (12mm) seam allowances.

1. Cut 2 pieces of spandex 2½˝ (6.4cm) wide by the length of your neck measurement on the pattern plus 1˝ (2.5cm) for the collar.

2. Refer to your pattern pieces and cut 1 torso back on the fabric fold, eliminating the seam allowance.

3. Add ½˝ (12mm) seam allowance to the center front of the torso front and cut 2 fabric pieces, instead of placing the piece on the fabric fold.

4. With right sides together, sew the 2 collar pieces together along the top long edge and the short side edges. Turn the collar right side out and press. *figs A & B*

5. Pin the collar to the right side of the bodysuit and sew in place. *fig C*

6. Sew the zipper in the back opening, extending the zipper through the finished short edges of the collar.

TIP *To add a back zipper and collar to the bodysuit, cut 1 torso front on the fold, add ½˝ to the center of the torso back pieces and cut 2 pieces. Follow the same instructions for the collar as in the front zipper and collar instructions (page 96).*

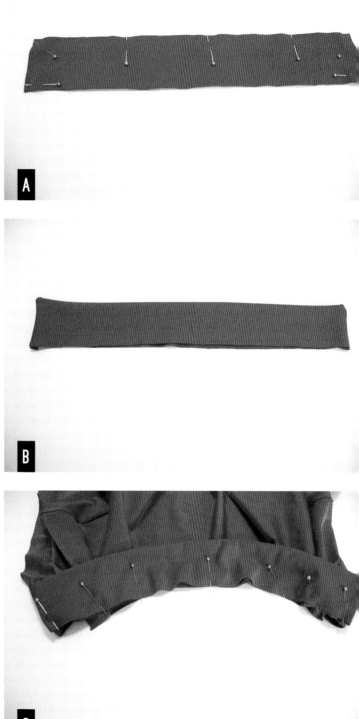

Neckline Variations

The neckline of a bodysuit can change for comfort, style, and/or aesthetics. If you are looking for screen accuracy, you will likely need to modify most necklines to achieve your desired outcome.

The first step for creating new necklines is to determine if your zipper will be in the front or the back of your bodysuit. Once you know where you want your zipper, mark the neckline placement either directly on the mock-up or on the torso pattern piece before cutting out the fashion fabric for your project. Most often, you will finish the neckline before inserting the zipper.

V-NECKLINE FRONT ZIPPER

1. Cut 1 torso back on the fabric fold and add seam allowance to the center front of the torso front pattern and cut 2.

2. Decide how deep you want the V-neckline; they are typically between 3˝ (7.6cm) and 6˝ (15.2cm) deep. Measure the desired depth down the center front seamline to mark the placement of the zipper.

3. Draw a new neckline by connecting the center front marking to the neckline curve or to the shoulder seam. *fig A*

4. Fold the neckline edges ½˝ (12mm) to the wrong side and sew.

5. Baste the center front seam and insert the zipper, following the instructions on the zipper packaging for a centered application.

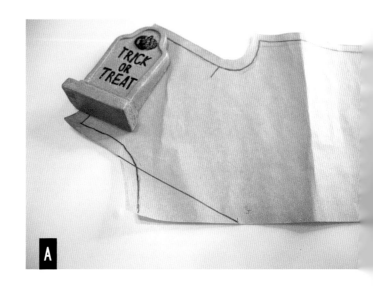

A

Hoods

Hoods are a great addition to a bodysuit. They can be used to add intrigue to a character. In this section, I will show you how to make a two-piece hood and a three-piece hood. These pieces work best with a front zipper and any kind of neckline except one with a collar.

TWO-PIECE HOOD

You will need ½ yard (45.7m) of spandex. Use a stretch stitch (page 32).

1. Make a paper pattern for the hood by duplicating the illustration, using a ruler and French curve to draw the lines. Measurements include ½″ (12mm) seam allowances.

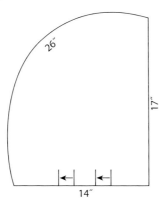

2. Cut 2 hood pieces from spandex.

3. With right sides together, sew the hood pieces together along the curved edges. *fig B*

4. Fold the front edge ½″ (12mm) to the wrong side and sew the hem. *fig C*

5. Pinch the fabric at the neckline markings to form 4 small pleats. Baste across the folds in the seam allowance.

6. With right sides together, sew the hood to the neckline of the bodysuit before adding the zipper.

7. Understitch the hood and neckline seam (page 32).

TIP *Lengthening and shortening the height of the hood changes how it sits on your shoulders. Shortening the hood makes it fit tighter and closer to the face. Lengthening it adds drama and drape.*

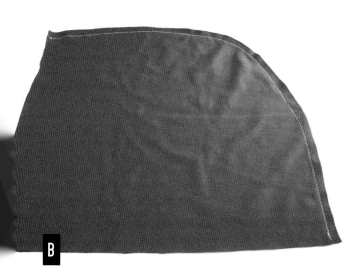

B

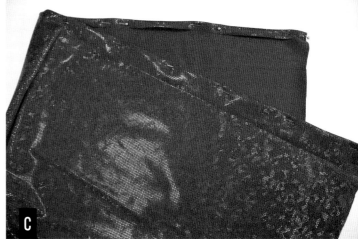

C

THREE-PIECE HOOD

You will need ½ yard (45.7m) of spandex. Use a stretch stitch (page 32).

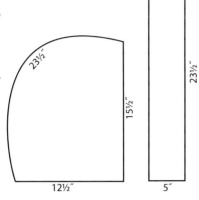

1. Make paper patterns for the hood by duplicating the illustration, using a ruler and French curve to draw the lines. Measurements include ½″ (12mm) seam allowances.

2. Cut 1 middle piece and 2 side pieces.

3. Sew a side piece to each side of the middle piece. *fig D*

4. Hem the front edge of the hood by pressing ½″ (12mm) to the wrong side and stitching. *fig E*

5. Follow the finishing instructions for the Two-Piece Hood, Steps 5–7 (page 99).

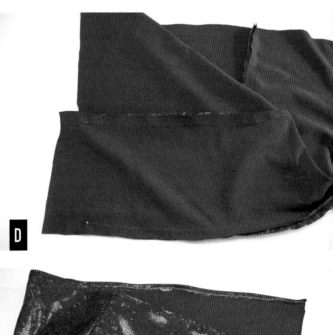

D

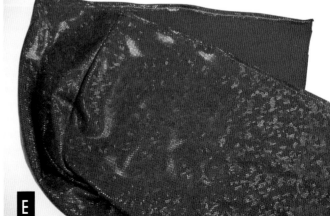

E

Sleeves

Sleeve lengths and styles often change from costume to costume. To make your life easier, you can use your bodysuit mock-up to find and test the placement of different-length and different-style sleeves. Keep the various sleeve mock-up variations as well as the paper patterns, so you always have already fitted sleeve options. Write notes on the paper patterns if you want to remember details.

THREE-QUARTER SLEEVES

You will need ½ yard (45.7m) of spandex. Use ½˝ (12mm) seam allowances.

1. Make these modifications directly on your mock-up sleeve or on the pattern if you prefer. Measure your arm from your shoulder to just past your elbow to determine the sleeve length. *fig A*

2. Remove the sleeve from the bodysuit with a seam ripper and open the underarm seam as well. *fig B*

3. Use the measurement from Step 1 to mark the new length on the mock-up sleeve. Add ½″ (12mm) hem allowance. Draw a straight line across the sleeve and cut along the new hemline *fig C*

4. Fold the bottom edge ½″ (12mm) to the wrong side and sew the hem. *fig D*

5. Sew the underarm seam with right sides together.

6. Reattach the new sleeve to the bodysuit.

C

D

SHORT SLEEVES

You will need ½ yard (45.7m) of spandex. Use ½″ (12mm) seam allowances.

1. Measure your arm from the shoulder to just past your elbow. *fig E*

2. To finish, refer to Three-Quarter Sleeves, Steps 2–6 (page 101).

E

Sleeveless

You will need the mock-up bodysuit to mark up for future sleeveless bodysuits (see Build Your Own Bodysuit, page 88.)

1. Take a sleeve off the bodysuit with a seam ripper.

2. Mark the bodysuit ¾″ (19mm) away from the armhole seam. *fig A*

3. Trim the sleeve opening to this marking.

4. Fold the armhole edges ½″ (12mm) to the wrong side and sew the hem. *fig B*

NOTE ◆ *The sleeveless option can cut in toward the neck, making the shoulder seam narrower, as much as you would like. Be sure to start wider and then mark it narrower after you see how it looks. Sleeveless with a V-neck or scoop neck might also need trimming from the seam closer to the neck if a super-thin shoulder strap is desired.*

A

B

Topstitching Details

Topstitching is a stitch that is meant to be seen but can also have quite a bit of functionality. While decorative stitches like flowers and bows are cute and work well for petticoats and bloomers, they don't allow for the best movement and stretch in spandex. Topstitching, on the other hand, is just a straight stitch that can be done next to the seam and that will permanently fold the seam allowance in a particular direction. This can be useful when working with very sheer fabrics when you don't want the seam to be seen through the fabric. Using a contrasting thread color that might appear in another part of the costume can also create a nice decorative touch. Alternatively, the overlock machine has a decorative stretch stitch called the flatlock stitch. It can be stitched with two or three different color threads for a bit of fun.

MAKE A COLOR-BLOCKED BODYSUIT

Color blocking is used quite often in superhero costumes like Jean Grey or Rouge (from Marvel's classic X-Men), as well as on bodysuits that can be worn under armor. The purpose of color blocking can be to enhance the shape of a figure, play with texture, or just to look more aesthetically pleasing. Color blocking can be as complicated or as easy as you would like it to be. Remember color blocking isn't necessarily just changing the color of fabric blocks, it can be different textured fabrics and even the same color of fabric but with different patterns or textures.

The best way to implement color blocking is to start with a bodysuit mock-up with the chosen sleeve length, leg length, neckline, and zipper placement. Fabric choice plays a large part in the color blocking; while I have already discussed spandex, there's also nude illusion fabric which is a stretch fabric used in ice skating or dance costumes. This can come in a variety of colors and opacities, making some more see-through than others. When picking these kinds of fabrics, it is important to understand how the blocking placement will look with any underwear that you plan to wear under the bodysuit.

COSPLAYER: Jedimanda
COSTUME: Jean Grey from *X-Men*

Photography by Alexandra Lee Studios

Materials

- Bodysuit mock-up
- Fabric marking pen
- Permanent marker
- Scissors
- Straight ruler
- French curve
- Spandex (amount determined by your design)
- 16″–22″ (41–56cm) zipper
- Zipper foot

Make It

Use a stretch stitch (page 32).

1. Turn the bodysuit mock-up inside out, and with the marker, mark every original seamline.

This will help you avoid confusion when you start adding color block shapes.

2. Starting with the torso section, start marking color blocks with a ruler and fabric marking pen. It helps to have a vision before you start. I like to have one or more references nearby during this step to get the most accurate version of what I am going for. You might also want to sketch out (in color) the color blocking so you a sense of how the finished bodysuit will look. *fig A*

TIP · *If you have a dress form, use it to better see and measure the placement markings on the torso. You can also make the markings while wearing the bodysuit, especially if the color blocks are not perfectly shaped.*

A

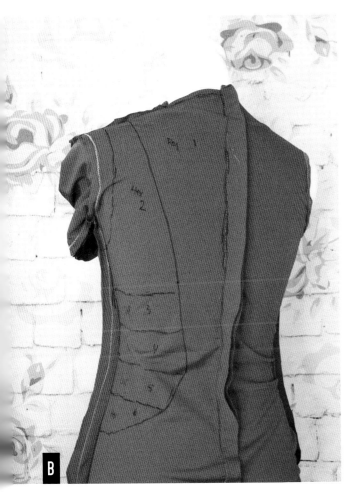

B

C

3. When you know the color block markings are in a good place and the design works, go over them with a marker. *fig B*

4. Label each piece based on color or fabric type and assign each of them a number. *fig C*

TIP

Take a picture of the marked and labeled bodysuit so you can refer to the piece numbers when you are ready to put the puzzle pieces back together.

5. You can mark the legs and arms while you are wearing the bodysuit, or if it is easier, place the bodysuit on a table to measure and mark. *fig D*

D

E

6. Seam rip the torso front, torso back, leg, sleeve, so there are 4 separate mock-up pieces.

7. Cut out the color block sections. *fig E*

8. Pin the color block sections to the respective fabrics. Pin them on the fold, if you need 2 pieces. If you planned an asymmetrical design, pin the pieces to 1 layer of fabric. *fig F*

9. Add ½˝ (12mm) seam allowances to the edges of the sections that do not already have a seam allowance. Because you marked the original seamlines on the sewn mock-up, you can tell which pieces already have the seam allowance. *fig G*

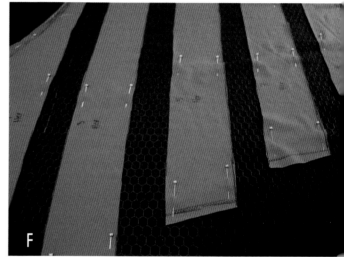

F

G

10. Referring to the numbers, sew the pieces back together. To do this, focus on a larger piece, like the arm or leg pieces, at a time. *fig H*

11. Once all the color block sections are sewn, join the finished pieces (arm, leg, torso front, torso back) together as you would normally sew them to make the bodysuit. *fig I*

EXTRA COSPLAY COMPONENTS

The devil is in the details and sometimes those details are the little extra bits you make. They can also make your costume more comfortable, which is very important.

Corset Covers

Since corsets are often used in cosplay not only to define a narrow waist but for attaching armor or even extensions like wings, they can become an eyesore if seen. You could create a new corset to match every set of armor you make, but that becomes expensive and time consuming. Most bodysuits are made of spandex, and I would not recommend making a corset out of spandex. So instead of creating a new corset every time you make a new costume, you could use the same corset each time and just become proficient in hiding it.

A common way to hide a corset is simply to wear it under your bodysuit. This works in quite a few cases and can be the easier fix if you're in a pinch. However, there are a few reasons why wearing a corset under a bodysuit isn't the best way to hide it. First, if you're wearing your corset under your bodysuit, you still need something to wear under the corset to protect your skin. A tank top works just fine but wearing a tank top, a corset, and then the bodysuit can feel like a lot. Wearing your corset under your bodysuit also means that you won't be able to attach anything to it without having to create holes in bodysuit for details or attachments to be visible on the outside of the bodysuit. This added engineering step can be daunting, and it is not necessary.

Instead, a spandex corset cover is an easy garment that can be made in about an hour and allows full access to the corset. If you can, just wear your corset on top of your bodysuit, and you won't need a chemise. You can even make it match the rest of the bodysuit or create fun details on it that your bodysuit already has. A corset cover gives you all the accessibility of the corset for adding wings, tails, or any kind of extension you want.

COSPLAYER: Casey Renee Cosplay
COSTUME: Stellagosa from *World of Warcraft* video game
Photography by Alexandra Lee Studios

MAKE A CORSET COVER

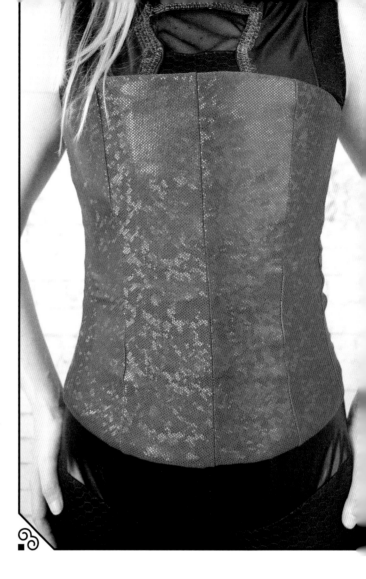

Materials

- ¾ yard (68.6cm) of spandex to match your bodysuit
- 10″–18″ (25.4–45.7cm) of 1″ (2.5cm)-wide hook-and-loop tape

Pattern Prep and Cutting

A full-size download of the corset pattern is available; see Downloadable Patterns (page 30) for the link.

Add ½″ (12mm) extra seam allowance to the straight edges of the center front and center back panel patterns. The goal of the corset cover is to fit over the corset, so it needs to overlap in the back to make that happen. **fig A**

Add 2″ (5.1cm) of extra fabric to the top and the bottom of all the panel patterns. This extra length allows the top and bottom edges to fold over and tuck into the corset. **fig B**

SPANDEX
Cut 2 each of Center Front, Side Front, Side, Side Back, and Back panels.

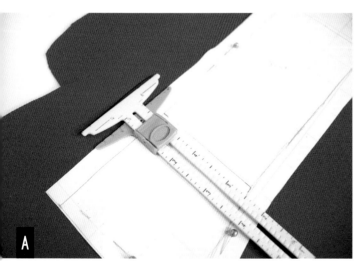

A

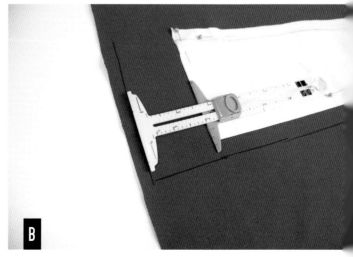

B

Make It

Use a stretch stitch (page 32).

1. Sew the center front panels together. Sew the side front panels to the center front panels.

2. Sew the side back pieces to the center back panels.

3. Sew the side panels to the joined center front/side front and center back/side back pieces to join the all the panels, leaving the center back open.

4. Fold the center back edge ½˝ (12mm) to the wrong side and sew.

5. Fold the top and bottom edges ½˝ (12mm) to the wrong side and sew. *fig C*

6. Try on the cover over the corset to mark the placement for the hook-and-loop tape.

7. Sew the tape pieces in place. *fig D*

C

D

Playing with Gender

The concept of dressing up as another gender is not new. Cosplaying a different gender than you identify as is another great way to share your artistry and love for a fandom. Padding and compression can be used to help create these illusions.

Padding

Padding is commonly used to enhance the hips and buttocks. Padding is typically shaped from high-density foam, available in various thicknesses and sizes, using an electric knife or even a bread knife. The goal is to carve into the foam so that the middle of the pad is the thickest with the edges tapered. Creating a set of hip pads that are even on both sides, smooth, and proportionate to the waist and chest can take a few tries to get right, however the padding paired with a pair of dance tights can create the illusion of full hips. The same works to create a full butt!

Foam padding isn't as good at enhancing breasts; instead, chest plates create a better full-bust illusion and are readily available for purchase online. There have been some cosplayers who have made their chest plates, but it is not very common.

Compression

While padding adds shape, compression creates a non-binary, masculine, or gender fluid illusion. There are a couple of ways to accomplish chest binding. Please note that all the following suggestions are for short-term binding. Never use duct tape or plastic wrap to bind and if you're new to binding, it's important to take breaks and avoid binding on consecutive days.

First, try a sports bra; this is an easy option, especially if you're cosplaying a character that wears larger clothes or layers of clothes. Alternatively, you can purchase professional-grade binders that are medically approved to be used for binding. If you plan to do a lot of binding, this is the best option.

For open chest binding, try TransTape. This tape is meant to be used on your skin, but you should properly wash and dry your chest before applying. The purpose of open chest binding is to create a look that can be worn with an open shirt or lower cut shirt. There are quite a few how-to tutorials online. For the best results, combine this with contouring makeup on the chest.

Leggings and Shorts

It's so easy to copy a pair of shorts or leggings you already own to make your very own pair to wear under your garments.

Make a Basic Leggings and Shorts Pattern

Trace a pair of your own leggings or shorts to make the pattern.

1. Turn the leggings or shorts wrong side out and put one leg inside the other leg.

2. Lay the leggings flat with the leg inseam lined up and trace the front crotch curve, inseam, waistline, and hem onto a pattern or craft paper. *fig A*

3. Place a pin along the leg outer edge as reference for the center front/back of the leg and mark the pin location on the paper.

4. Using the pin placement, flip the leggings over, so the outer edge of the leggings aligns with the outer edge of the pattern. Mark the leg inseam, the back crotch curve, the bottom hem, and the top edge of the leggings. This creates one full leg pattern piece.

5. Add ½˝ (13mm) seam allowance to the crotch curves and inseams.

6. Add ½˝ (12mm) hem allowance to the bottom edge if you have traced leggings; add 1˝ (2.5mm) hem allowance if you have traced shorts.

7. There are two ways to finish the waist: add a waistband or create a casing for elastic. Refer to the waist finish of the leggings or shorts you are tracing.

The author's undergarments for her Sakizou Amethyst cosplay, made for modesty and comfort onstage.

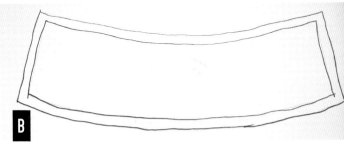

- For a separate waistband, lay the leggings out flat and trace the front or back waistband. Add ½˝ (12mm) seam allowance to all the edges. *fig B*

- For an elastic casing, add 1½˝ (3.8mm) to the top edge.

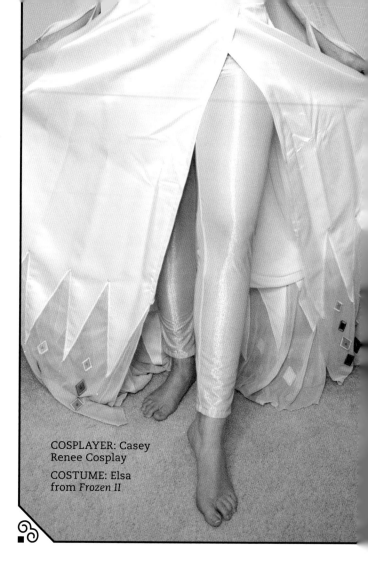

◆MAKE LEGGINGS

These leggings feature a 5″ (12.7mm) wide waistband.

Materials

- 1–1½ yards (91.4–1.4m) of spandex
- 1–2 yards (91.4–5.1m) of 1″ (2.5cm)-wide elastic

Cutting

SPANDEX

Cut 2 leg pieces and 4 waistband pieces.

ELASTIC

Measure your waist and add 1″ (2.5mm). Cut to the measurement.

COSPLAYER: Casey Renee Cosplay

COSTUME: Elsa from *Frozen II*

Make the Leggings

Use a stretch stitch (page 32).

Waistband

1. With right sides together, sew the side edges of 2 waistband pieces. Repeat with the remaining 2 waistband pieces. ***fig A***

A

2. With right sides together, sew the separate waistband pieces together at the top edge, aligning the side seams. *fig B*

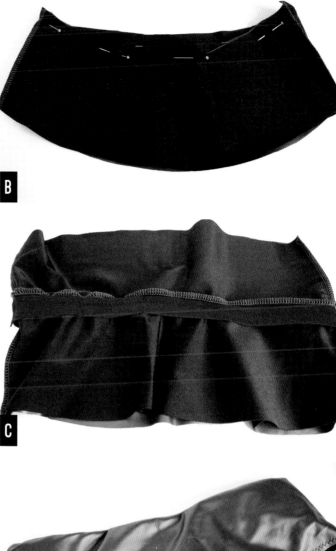

3. Overlap the ends of the elastic 1˝ (2.5cm) and sew together.

4. Pin the elastic to the inside of the waistband at the side seams. Sew to the waistband, stretching the elastic as you sew. *fig C*

5. Sew the waistband layers together at the bottom edge. *fig D*

Leggings

1. With the right sides together, sew the inseam of each leg piece.

2. Place one leg inside the other with right sides together and sew the curved crotch seam.

3. Pull the leg to the outside; with right sides together, sew the waistband to the legs. *fig E*

4. Fold the bottom edges ½˝ (12mm) to the wrong side and sew the hem.

◆MAKE SHORTS

These shorts feature an elastic casing.

Materials

- ¾ yard (69cm) of spandex
- 1–2 yards (2.5cm) of 1˝ (2.5cm)-wide elastic

Cutting

SPANDEX

Cut 2 leg pieces.

ELASTIC

Measure your waist and add 1˝ (2.5mm). Cut to the measurement.

Make the Shorts

Use a stretch stitch (page 32).

1. With right sides together, sew the inseam of each leg piece. *fig A*

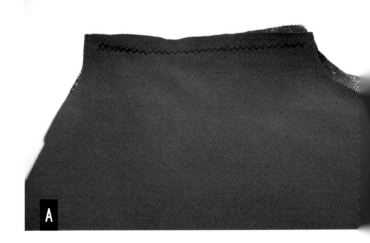

A

2. Fold the bottom edges 1˝ (2.5mm) to the wrong side and sew the hem. *fig B*

3. Place one leg inside the other with right sides together and sew the curved crotch seam. *fig C*

4. Fold the top of the waistband 1½˝ (3.8cm) to the wrong side and sew close to the raw edge, leaving a 2˝ (5.1cm) opening in the back.

5. Feed the elastic through the opening using a safety pin. *fig D*

6. Overlap the elastic 1˝ (2.5cm) and sew the ends together.

7. Sew the opening closed.

B

C

D

Cowl

Some costumes have fancy helmets or head wear that could benefit from protection from sweat or oils produced by your hair. A cowl is the perfect garment to be worn between a helmet and hair. It can also hide your hair if there is no visible hair on the character you are portraying.

◆MAKE A COWL

Materials

- ½ yard (45.7m) of spandex
- Fabric marking pen or tailor's chalk

Pattern Prep and Cutting

A full-size download of the cowl pattern is available; see Downloadable Patterns (page 30) for the link.

SPANDEX

Cut 2 cowl pieces. Transfer the dart markings to the wrong side of the fabric pieces.

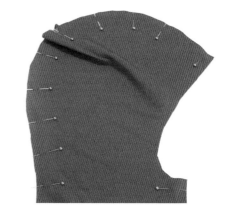

B

Make It

Use ½˝ (12mm) seam allowances. Use a stretch stitch (page 32).

1. Sew the darts on each piece. Press.

2. With right sides together, sew the cowl pieces together on the center curved seam and the center front seam. *fig A*

3. Fold the front edges ½˝ (12mm) to the wrong side and sew. *fig B*

4. Fold the bottom edge ½˝ (12mm) to the wrong side and sew the hem. *fig C*

NOTE ◆ *If you would like to tuck the hood into your bodysuit, simply lengthen the bottom edge of the cowl.*

C

G

Wristlets with Pockets

One of the hardest parts about cosplay is finding places to put your stuff while in costume. Not everyone has a gown they can sew eighteenth-century style pockets into that can carry an entire lunch. So, finding places to hide the couple of things you might have to access a lot is extremely helpful. There are many places you can naturally hide things, like in a boot or women in their bras, or in functional pouches if that is something true to your costume design. You can hide your phone in a quiver or even ask your friend to carry a backpack and help you out throughout the day. But there are still two things that I almost never want to find myself without on the convention floor, and that is my badge and money. Way back in the day, when I used to cosplay Tauriel (an elf from *The Hobbit* series), I would hide some cash and my badge right in my wristlets. They were form-fitting but not secure, so if I took them off without paying attention, my money would fall all over the place. Adding a pocket to the wristlet will prevent that from happening. The pocket might not be large enough for a phone, although if you don't mind the bulky look of it, it might just work for you. You can place the pocket on the outside or inside of the wristlet.

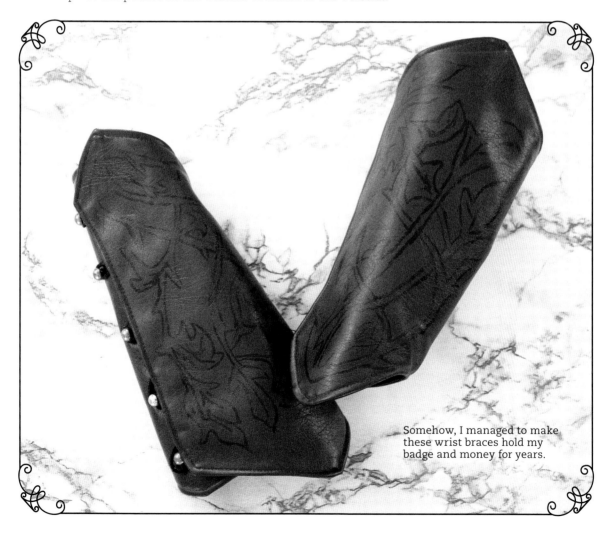

Somehow, I managed to make these wrist braces hold my badge and money for years.

MAKE WRISTLETS

Materials

- ½ yard (45.7cm) of spandex
- Pattern or craft paper
- 2 sets of snaps (*optional*)

Pattern Prep and Cutting

Draw a trapezoid using the following measurements: A = forearm measurement; B = Distance from top of forearm to wrist; C = wrist measurement

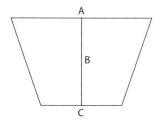

Add ¾" (19mm) seam allowance on all edges.

SPANDEX

Cut 4 wristlet pieces.

Make It

Use a stretch stitch (page 32).

1. With right sides together, sew the top and bottom edges of each wristlet, leaving half of the top seam open, as shown. *fig A*

2. Turn the pieces right side out, then top-stitch along each of the top seams separately. Don't topstitch through the opening, since the opening is for the pocket. *fig B*

3. With right sides together, fold each wristlet in half and sew the side edges. *fig C*

4. Hand sew snaps inside the edges at the opening to hold the pocket closed; this is optional.

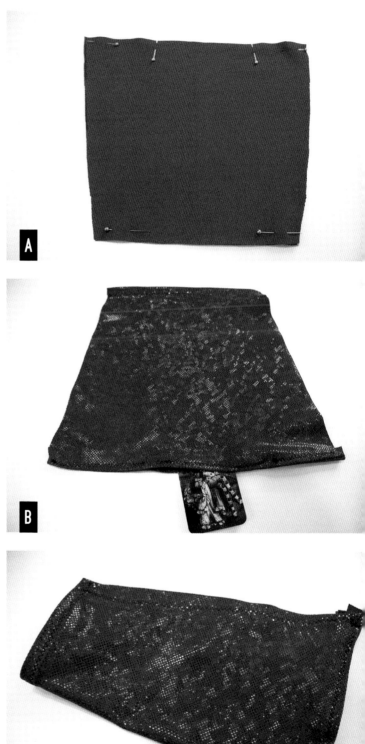

ARMOR ATTACHMENTS

It seems that cosplayers have found many ways to attach armor to themselves throughout the years. There is no wrong way to get your armor on and to keep it on, however some ways can make your life easier while you are wearing your costume. Since you are going the extra lengths to create a custom bodysuit, it is a good idea to customize just exactly how and where attachments go. Figuring out which attachments are going to work best for you is part of the process of making your armor, and it is very important to have your armor pieces made before placing any attachments. However, it never hurts to plan and discover what works best for your project.

Hook-and-Loop Tape

This product is actually two tapes; on one side there are tiny scratchy hooks, and on the other, there are softer loops that stick to the hooks when pressed together. It comes in many different widths and lengths and in every color of the rainbow. Hook-and-loop tape even comes with an adhesive on the back, but the adhesive can gunk up your sewing machine needle. I highly recommend using the sew-in version since it allows for more possibilities. It can be sewn in, but it can also be glued onto the inside of an armor piece or even onto fabric if needed.

At this point, the order of operations becomes a bit tricky. You'll want to figure out the perfect placement for each piece in a certain location so that the attachments don't run into each other. Many sewing machines allow you to remove the extension table, making the machine a free-arm to make it easier to sew sleeve and leg pieces. Alternatively, you can hand sew the hook-and-loop tape in place using a backstitch (page 34), but this is pretty time consuming.

To machine sew hook-and-loop tape to a bodysuit, use a 1.5mm to 2mm stitch length. Sew on the edges then stitch an X for a strong bond to the fabric. However, this can be very tricky to do when the bodysuit is already sewn. The next best thing would be to sew the long edges and then straight through the center. Make sure that you backstitch at the beginning and end of every stitch line to fully secure the pieces to your bodysuit.

COSPLAYER: altf4cosplay
COSTUME: Monster Hunter
from *Monster Hunter*

*Photography by Alexandra Lee
Studios*

Magnets

Another great way to attach the armor to your bodysuit is with magnets. Magnets come in multiple strengths and, therefore, can be good for lightweight or heavyweight pieces of armor. Sometimes you will want to use several magnets to place and hold a larger or heavier piece of armor. The placement of magnets is very important and using more magnets to make sure a piece stays on is a much better decision than not using enough magnets. The best type of magnets for cosplay are neodymium magnets; they are very strong and come in various sizes.

There are two basic ways to attach magnets to your bodysuit. Using hot glue is a very quick and easy way to attach magnets and can be done once the suit is finished or while you are still making it. Attaching magnets close to the perimeter of each armor piece allows for the best bond. Hot glue is a good way to set magnets into your armor all at the same time.

This is an example of securing an attachment to a corset with magnets. The costume is the Red Queen from Wasteland Alice, concept art created by SKS Props.

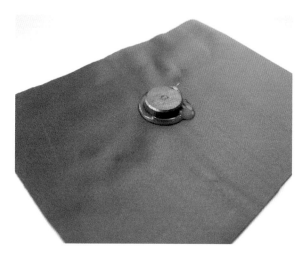

The downside to using hot glue is that some fabrics have a glossy finish which tends to repel the hot glue. There are lots of PVC-type spandex and faux leathers that essentially eliminate hot glue as an option.

If you can't use hot glue, try creating a magnet-sized pocket at the desired location. You will need to plan ahead for this attachment method. I like to cut squares of fabric that match my bodysuit, about twice the size of the magnet. Since spandex doesn't fray, I just hand stitch the fabric square down, leaving an opening at the top to drop my magnet in, and then sew the top closed. This can also be done by machine, but once the bodysuit is sewn, it gets a bit more difficult to sew pockets for magnets where they are needed.

Turn Your Scraps into Straps

While hook-and-loop tape and magnets are great tools, sometimes the easiest way to attach armor to a bodysuit is with straps. Straps can be used both with the tape and magnets or on their own. Using straps just by themselves can cause some issues with the armor pieces moving in certain places, like your legs, so make sure to do some movement tests wearing your armor before the convention day. Straps can be made of leather, nylon straps with plastic buckles, or even elastic. Depending on the costume design and aesthetic, elastic strips or nylon straps might be an eyesore while wearing your cosplay. If you can't find elastic in the right color, find something to blend in with the bodysuit. Considering that you just spent all this time making a great bodysuit out of custom fabric, you don't want the straps to be the thing that weighs you down. A great way you can remedy this is by making covers for your straps out of fabric scraps from your bodysuit. Since the sewing and fabric-making industry creates quite a bit of waste, this is a great way to cut back on the amount of fabric waste you create in your cosplay shop.

To make strap covers, measure and cut the elastic or nylon strap first. Then measure and cut the fabric length, allowing extra for gathers so the strap can stretch. From there, lay your strap onto the fabric and trace around it, adding about ½″ (12mm) seam allowance on the lengthwise sides; there's no need for seam allowance on the ends. Cut 2 of these pieces and sew them with right sides together using a zigzag stitch. Turn them right side out and then feed through the elastic or strap using a safety pin as your guide. Then, sew the ends of the cover to the ends of the elastic or strap so that the cover can't slide up and down. Now you have fabulous camouflage straps to go with your brand-new bodysuit.

Wardrobe Extensions

Corsets are an excellent base for the harness systems that hold up wings or other extensions for cosplay. Having a harness system and solid base is important for a couple of reasons. First, a harness helps distribute the weight of the extension. Wings, for instance, can be very heavy, and if you don't have a system in place to distribute their weight, you will likely have issues wearing the costume for long periods of time. Second, a harness helps control the movement of extensions like wings or a tail, so they move with you.

COSPLAYER: PaisleyandGlue
COSTUME: Maleficent from *Maleficent*
Photography by Alexandra Lee Studios

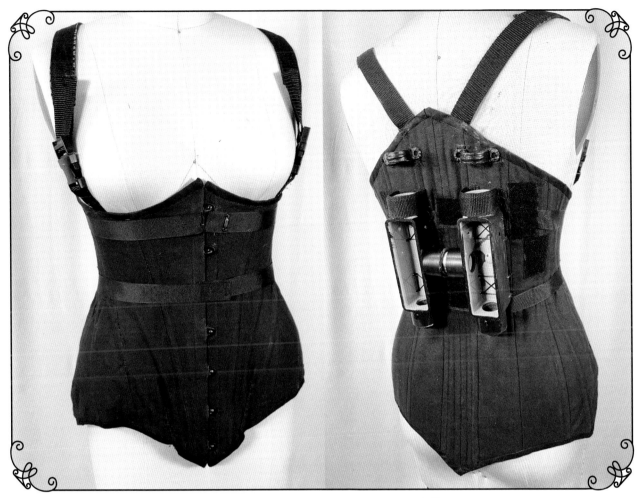

Front (left) and back (right) of harness worn under Maleficent costume

Photography by PaisleyandGlue

There are several ways to modify a corset to make it work for your costume. Maggie from Paisley and Glue sewed a harness into her corset to hold her Maleficent wings. She modified her corset so there is a busk in the front without lacing to ensure that the corset has enough structure to hold the weight of the wings. She also added tape at her waist and at her ribs that close in the front. These tapes, combined with padding inside her corset, kept the weight of the wings from pushing down onto her hips.

Maggie drilled holes in the plastic harness that the wings slide into and then used those holes to stitch the harness onto the back of the corset.

She also stitched nylon straps with parachute buckles onto the back of the corset, near the top. The straps rest on her shoulders and connect at the front of the corset. This added a third area to help distribute and carry the weight of the wings, and it prevents the wings from falling backward while she wears the harness. When she walks forward, the wings move with her as if she had wings.

CARE AND STORAGE

Can You Wash That?

Time to play my favorite game—can you wash that? In cosplay, we wear a lot of interesting garments to a lot of interesting places. We often have encounters that are not always planned, from being outside in the rain during a photoshoot or spilling cheese sauce on yourself. These kinds of accidents can be difficult to avoid, so are all these undergarments that we just spent weeks making washable?

The answer is that some of them are.

The purpose of the chemise and bloomers is to collect the body oils and sweat produced while wearing the garment to keep the corset as clean as possible. So, these two garments are completely safe to machine wash, with hot water and detergent. The key to keeping these garments from shrinking in the first wash is to prewash your fabric before making your garments. Adding a little bit of fabric softener will keep the garments smelling delicious and lasting longer.

As for your corset, it should not be machine washed for any reason. The washing machine can damage the steel. After taking your corset off, lay it open flat with the lining side up. Even though the chemise will soak up most of your sweat, there might be some that makes it to the corset, so it needs to air out. Corsets do not need to be cleaned often, but there are a few things you can do to help keep them lasting a long time. If your corset starts to smell, you can

lightly spray or dab the inside with a mixture of equal parts vodka and water. Take care, since some fabrics can be stained by the vodka mixture. An antibacterial Febreze product is also an option for spraying on the inside and eliminating odor. If you eventually get something on your corset, try spot cleaning it with Borax; just do a tiny spot test to see how it reacts with your fabric.

It just so happens that while I was outside photographing the hoop skirt for this very book, it got dirty as I sat on my stool. You can get some stains out of hoop skirts with a washcloth, warm water, and hand soap.

Taking care of your petticoat is a little easier than you would expect. You can hand wash it, or machine wash it. Washing it with detergent is safe, but refrain from adding detergents with bleach or any bleach products, for these can break down the fibers.

For machine washing, make sure to use a warm and delicate machine setting. If there are any stains left on the petticoat when the wash cycle is done, you can spot clean them with a washcloth and detergent. Finally, to dry your petticoat, turn it inside out and lay it flat on top of a couple of towels, spreading it out as wide as you can. Avoid hanging the garment to dry because the water can create added weight and pull down at the petticoat. You can put the petticoat in the dryer for a few minutes on a low heat setting to get it to fluff up again.

Hand wash bodysuits and spandex items in lukewarm water with a little bit of detergent. This will keep the spandex from stretching too much and warping out of shape.

Storage

Storing the chemise, bloomers, and spandex items is as easy as folding them and putting them in a drawer once they are completely dry.

After taking off the corset, allow it to lay flat with the lining side up until it is completely dry. From there, fold the corset in half and store it flat. It is not good for the bones and the structure of the corset to roll it up and tie it.

You can also hang the corset over a hanger by the lacing, ensuring that the weight is distributed on both sides. The key to storing corsets is to avoid pressure on the boning.

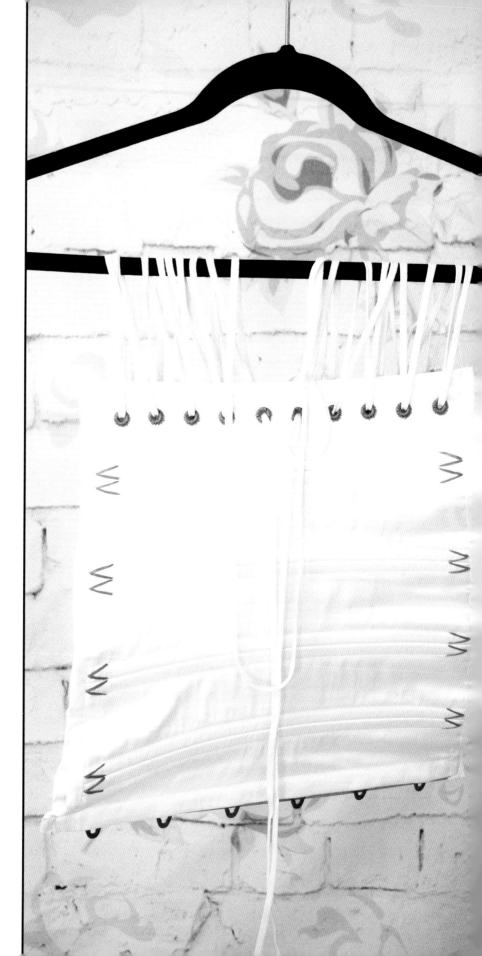

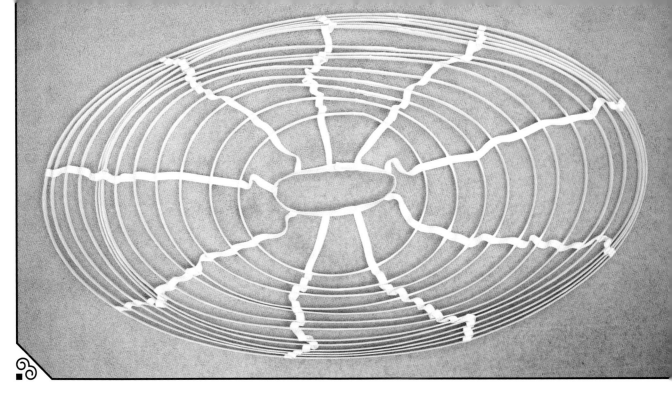

Storing hoop skirts is similar to storing corsets in the sense that you don't want to put too much pressure on the boning or the structures can warp out of shape. You can store your hoopskirt flat under your bed. Just make sure to store it in a bag of some kind so that it doesn't collect dust and dirt. Hoops can also be stored in a bag hanging on a hanger in your closet if you have closet space. Alternatively, you can store your hoop on your wall like a wall decoration. I like to store hoops this way while I am constructing gowns to go over them; since they take up so much space on my dress form.

To store petticoats, roll them up. Start at the waistband and roll it until it can't anymore. Then put it in a bag and store it that way. You can temporarily store petticoats by hanging them on a hanger, although they take up quite a lot of space, and over time they can lose their puffiness.

GLOSSARY

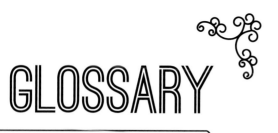

This is a glossary of historical undergarments. The terms in this section of the book should be a jumping-off point for future undergarment needs.

TIP When researching historical garments, make sure to check multiple sources.

BLOOMERS   Loose-fitting underpants, gathered at the knee, for women and girls. They were worn in the Victorian and Edwardian eras.

BODIES   Boned undergarment for the torso; precursor to stays; became popular in the Tudor era; created a conical shape. Worn in the sixteenth and seventeenth centuries.

BRA   Undergarment worn by women to support the breasts.

BUM PADS   Stuffed pad tied around the waist to give extra shape to the buttocks; worn in the eighteenth and nineteenth centuries.

BUM ROLL   Crescent-shaped pad worn under ladies' skirts in the sixteenth and seventeenth centuries.

BUSTLE HOOP   Victorian-era steel hoop structure designed to be worn behind the body to hold many pounds of skirt material.

CAGE CRINOLINE   Victorian-era hoop skirt made out of steel hoops typically 110˝ (280cm) or wider at the bottom.

CHEMISE   Loose-fitting undergarment, made of linen or cotton, worn during the daytime or to sleep in.

COMBINATION UNDERWEAR   This is a chemise and drawers combined into one garment; worn from the 1870s until the 1920s.

CORSET   A garment worn to shape the torso to help create the desired silhouette; popular from the 1830s until the 1920s.

CORSET COVER   Like a modern camisole, a corset cover smooths out the lines of the corset; worn in the 1860s through the Edwardian era.

CRINOLINE   Stiffened or hooped skirt to make a long skirt stand out; worn in the 1840s to 1850s. Also known as the fabric used to make a crinoline.

ELLIPTICAL CRINOLINE   Cage crinoline with an oval shape towards the back; used in 1860s ball gowns.

FRENCH/WHEEL FARTHINGALE   Rigid structure used by women in the sixteenth century to support their skirts; Queen Elizabeth I wore one.

GAMBESON Padded defensive jacket worn as armor separately or combined with mail or plate armor; worn as early as the fourth century BC until the seventeenth century.

GRAND PANNIER   Wide hoop structure worn over the hips in the eighteenth century, typically these were 4 feet (1.22m) or wider.

JUMP   A bodice women wore under their dresses in the eighteenth century, typically quilted instead of boned, and worn instead of stays.

LOINCLOTH   Simple piece of cloth wrapped around the hips, typically worn by men in hot countries. First known form of underwear.

PETTICOAT   Type of undergarment worn under a skirt or dress; this garment has changed vastly over the years but has been worn since at least the sixteenth century.

TIP | *The best way to find out what a garment looked like in a specific era or time period, search "era" + "garment" online (example: 1890s petticoat).*

POCKET PANNIERS   Basket-shaped, hoop-like garment worn on the hips; the pocket pannier was smaller than the grand pannier and was worn throughout the eighteenth century.

POCKETS   Historically, these refer to the pockets from the eighteenth century that were worn under dresses and were separate from the rest of the garment.

QUILTED PETTICOAT   A petticoat quilted for warmth, worn by most classes during the eighteenth century. Sometimes they were embroidered.

SHAPEWEAR   Women's tight-fitting underwear intended to control and shape the figure.

SLIP   Light dress (full slip) or skirt worn under a dress or skirt for modesty. These followed the chemise and became prevalent in the 1940s.

SPANISH FARTHINGALE   First version of the hoop skirt, a conical-shaped undergarment worn in the sixteenth and seventeenth centuries.

SPLIT BUM PADS   Two pads worn over the buttocks in eighteenth-century fashion to fill out the back area while wearing a pocket pannier or no hoop structure.

SPLIT DRAWERS   Also known as open drawers, these are pant-like underwear with an open crotch seam, worn in the nineteenth century and often were decorated with tucks and lace.

STAYS   Fully-boned, laced bodice worn underneath a gown (these came after bodies and before the corset), they were seen as from the late sixteenth century through the early nineteenth century.

STROPHIUM   Band of linen or leather folded and tucked around the chest to bind and reduce the size of women's breasts and worn in Ancient Greek and Roman times.

TUCKED PETTICOAT   A petticoat made with tucks or pintucks; this garment has been around in different forms since the eighteenth century.

TUNIC   Simple slip-on garment made with or without sleeves and usually knee-length or longer; worn as early as ancient Greek and Roman times; evolves slightly throughout time; still a garment worn today.

CHART 1 *Petticoat Cotton Circle Skirt and Flounce Measurements*

Petticoat lengths are based on the measurement from the hoop skirt waistband to the tenth hoop. All measurements are in inches.

FOR 36″ LENGTH

Waist	22	24	26	28	30	32	34	36	38	40	42	44	46	48	50	52	54
Waist radius	3¾	4	4¼	4½	5	5¼	5½	5¾	6¼	6½	6¾	7	7½	7¾	8	8½	8¾
Hem radius	39¾	40	40¼	40½	41	41¼	41½	41¾	42¼	42½	42¾	43	43½	43¾	44	44½	44¾
Flounce 1 length	625	630	633	638	643	650	653	658	665	670	672	675	683	688	693	700	705

FOR 37″ LENGTH

Waist	22	24	26	28	30	32	34	36	38	40	42	44	46	48	50	52	54
Waist radius	3¾	4	4¼	4½	5	5¼	5½	5¾	6¼	6½	6¾	7	7½	7¾	8	8½	8¾
Hem radius	40¾	41	41¼	41½	42	42¼	42½	42¾	43¼	43½	43¾	44	44½	44¾	45	45½	45¾
Flounce 1 length	640	643	650	653	660	665	670	672	680	683	688	693	700	705	708	715	720

FOR 38″ LENGTH

Waist	22	24	26	28	30	32	34	36	38	40	42	44	46	48	50	52	54
Waist radius	3¾	4	4¼	4½	5	5¼	5½	5¾	6¼	6½	6¾	7	7½	7¾	8	8½	8¾
Hem radius	41¾	42	42¼	42½	43	43¼	43½	43¾	44¼	44½	44¾	45	45½	45¾	46	46½	46¾
Flounce 1 length	658	660	665	670	675	680	683	688	698	700	705	708	715	720	725	733	735

FOR 39″ LENGTH

Waist	22	24	26	28	30	32	34	36	38	40	42	44	46	48	50	52	54
Waist radius	3¾	4	4¼	4½	5	5½	5¾	5¾	6¼	6½	6¾	7	7½	7¾	8	8½	8¾
Hem radius	42¾	43	43¼	43½	44	44¼	44½	44¾	45¼	45½	45¾	46	46½	46¾	47	47½	47¾
Flounce 1 length	672	675	680	683	693	690	700	705	713	715	720	725	733	735	740	748	753

FOR 40″ LENGTH

Waist	22	24	26	28	30	32	34	36	38	40	42	44	46	48	50	52	54
Waist radius	3¾	4	4¼	4½	5	5¼	5½	5¾	6½	6½	6¾	7	7½	7¾	8	8½	8¾
Hem radius	43¾	44	44¼	44½	45	45¼	45½	45¾	46¼	46½	46¾	47	47½	47¾	48	48½	48¾
Flounce 1 length	688	693	698	700	708	713	715	720	728	733	735	740	748	753	755	763	768

CHART 2 *Petticoat Organza Lower Tier and Flounce 2 Measurements*

Petticoat lengths are based on the measurement from the hoop skirt waistband to the tenth hoop. All measurements are in inches.

FOR 36″ LENGTH

Waist	22	24	26	28	30	32	34	36	38	40	42	44	46	48	50	52	54
Tier placement	27¾	28	28¼	28½	29	29¼	29½	29¾	30¼	30½	30¾	31	31½	31¾	32	32½	32¾
Tier width 14/length	348	352	356	358	364	368	370	374	380	384	386	390	396	398	402	408	412
Flounce 2 length	870	880	890	895	910	920	925	935	950	960	965	975	990	995	1005	1020	1030

FOR 37″ LENGTH

Waist	22	24	26	28	30	32	34	36	38	40	42	44	46	48	50	52	54
Tier placement	28½	28¾	29	29¼	29¾	30	30¼	30½	31	31¼	31½	31¾	32¼	32½	32¾	33½	33½
Tier width 14¼/length	358	360	364	366	374	376	380	382	388	392	396	398	404	408	410	418	420
Flounce 2 length	895	900	910	915	935	940	950	955	970	980	990	995	1010	1020	1025	1045	1050

FOR 38″ LENGTH

Waist	22	24	26	28	30	32	34	36	38	40	42	44	46	48	50	52	54
Tier placement	29¼	29½	29¾	30	30½	30¾	31	31¼	31½	32	32¼	32½	33	33¼	33½	34	34¼
Tier width 14½/length	366	370	372	376	382	386	388	392	398	400	404	408	414	416	420	426	430
Flounce 2 length	915	925	930	940	955	965	970	980	995	1000	1010	1020	1035	1040	1050	1065	1075

FOR 39″ LENGTH

Waist	22	24	26	28	30	32	34	36	38	40	42	44	46	48	50	52	54
Tier placement	29¾	30	30¼	30½	31	31¼	31½	31¾	32¼	32½	32¾	33	33½	33¾	34	34½	34¾
Tier width 15/length	374	376	380	384	390	392	396	400	406	408	412	414	420	424	428	434	436
Flounce 2 length	935	940	950	960	975	980	990	1000	1015	1020	1030	1035	1050	1060	1070	1085	1090

FOR 40″ LENGTH

Waist	22	24	26	28	30	32	34	36	38	40	42	44	46	48	50	52	54
Tier placement	30½	30¾	31	31¼	31¾	32	32¼	32½	33	33¼	33½	33¾	34¼	34½	34¾	35¼	35½
Tier width 15½/length	382	386	390	392	398	402	404	408	414	418	420	424	430	432	436	442	446
Flounce 2 length	955	965	975	980	995	1005	1010	1020	1035	1045	1050	1060	1075	1080	1090	1105	1115

CHART 3 *Petticoat Organza Upper Tier and Flounce 3 Measurements*

Petticoat lengths are based on the measurement from the hoop skirt waistband to the tenth hoop. All measurements are in inches.

FOR 36″ LENGTH

Waist	22	24	26	28	30	32	34	36	38	40	42	44	46	48	50	52	54
Tier placement	15¾	16	16¼	16½	17	17¼	17½	17¾	18¼	18½	18¾	19	19½	19¾	20	20½	20¾
Tier width 26/length	198	200	204	208	214	216	220	224	230	232	236	238	246	248	252	258	260
Flounce 3 length	495	500	510	520	535	540	550	560	575	580	590	595	615	620	630	645	650

FOR 37″ LENGTH

Waist	22	24	26	28	30	32	34	36	38	40	42	44	46	48	50	52	54
Tier placement	16¼	16½	16¾	17	17½	17¾	18	18¼	18¾	19	19¼	19½	20	20¼	20½	21	21¼
Tier width 26½/length	202	206	210	212	218	222	224	228	234	238	240	244	250	254	256	262	266
Flounce 3 length	505	515	525	530	545	555	560	570	585	595	600	610	625	635	640	655	665

FOR 38″ LENGTH

Waist	22	24	26	28	30	32	34	36	38	40	42	44	46	48	50	52	54
Tier placement	16½	16¾	17	17¼	17¾	18	18¼	18½	19	19¼	19½	19¾	20¼	20½	20¾	21¼	21½
Tier width 27¼/length	208	212	214	218	224	226	230	234	240	242	246	248	256	258	262	268	270
Flounce 3 length	520	530	535	545	560	565	575	585	600	605	615	620	635	645	655	670	675

FOR 39″ LENGTH

Waist	22	24	26	28	30	32	34	36	38	40	42	44	46	48	50	52	54
Tier placement	16¾	17	17¼	17½	18	18¼	18½	18¾	19¼	19½	19¾	20	20½	20¾	21	21½	21¾
Tier width 28/length	210	214	216	220	226	230	232	236	242	246	248	252	258	260	264	270	274
Flounce 3 length	525	535	540	550	565	575	580	590	605	615	620	630	645	650	660	675	685

FOR 40″ LENGTH

Waist	22	24	26	28	30	32	34	36	38	40	42	44	46	48	50	52	54
Tier placement	17¼	17½	17¾	18	18½	18¾	19	19¼	19¾	20	20¼	20½	21	21¼	21½	22	22¼
Tier width 2½/length	216	218	222	224	232	234	238	240	246	250	254	256	262	266	268	276	278
Flounce 3 length	540	545	555	560	580	585	595	600	615	625	635	640	655	665	670	690	695

CHART 4 *Petticoat Organza Circle Skirt and Flounce 4 Measurements*

Petticoat lengths are based on the measurement from the hoop skirt waistband to the 10th hoop. All measurements are in inches.

FOR 36″ LENGTH

Waist	22	24	26	28	30	32	34	36	38	40	42	44	46	48	50	52	54
Waist radius	3¾	4	4¼	4½	5	5¼	5½	5¾	6¼	6½	6¾	7	7½	7¾	8	8½	8¾
Hem radius	41¾	42	42¼	42½	43	43¼	43½	43¾	44¼	44½	44¾	45	45½	45¾	46	46½	46¾
Flounce 4 length	655	660	665	668	675	680	683	688	695	699	703	706	715	718	723	730	735

FOR 37″ LENGTH

Waist	22	24	26	28	30	32	34	36	38	40	42	44	46	48	50	52	54
Waist radius	3¾	4	4¼	4½	5	5¼	5½	5¾	6¼	6½	6¾	7	7½	7¾	8	8½	8¾
Hem radius	42¾	43	43¼	43½	44	44¼	44½	44¾	45¼	45½	45¾	46	46½	46¾	47	47½	47¾
Flounce 4 length	673	675	680	683	690	695	708	703	710	715	718	723	730	735	738	745	750

FOR 38″ LENGTH

Waist	22	24	26	28	30	32	34	36	38	40	42	44	46	48	50	52	54
Waist radius	3¾	4	4¼	4½	5	5¼	5½	5¾	6¼	6½	6¾	7	7½	7¾	8	8½	8¾
Hem radius	43¾	44	44¼	44½	45	45¼	45½	45¾	46¼	46½	46¾	47	47½	47¾	48	48½	48¾
Flounce 4 length	688	690	695	700	708	710	715	718	728	730	735	738	745	750	755	763	765

FOR 39″ LENGTH

Waist	22	24	26	28	30	32	34	36	38	40	42	44	46	48	50	52	54
Waist radius	3¾	4	4¼	4½	5	5¼	5½	5¾	6¼	6½	6¾	7	7½	7¾	8	8½	8¾
Hem radius	44¾	45	45¼	45½	46	46¼	46½	46¾	47¼	47½	47¾	48	48½	48¾	49	49½	49¾
Flounce 4 length	703	708	710	715	723	728	730	735	743	745	750	755	763	765	770	778	783

FOR 40″ LENGTH

Waist	22	24	26	28	30	32	34	36	38	40	42	44	46	48	50	52	54
Waist radius	3¾	4	4¼	4½	5	5¼	5½	5¾	6¼	6½	6¾	7	7½	7¾	8	8½	8¾
Hem radius	45¾	46	46¼	46½	47	47¼	47½	47¾	48¼	48½	48¾	49	49½	49¾	50	50½	50¾
Flounce 4 length	718	723	728	730	738	743	745	750	758	763	765	770	778	783	785	793	798

RESOURCES

ℰ Corsetry and Hoops

biasbespoke.com

burnleyandtrowbridge.com

corsetmaking.com

farthingalecorsetmakingsupplies.com

sewcurvy.com

ℰ Spandex

spandexhouse.com

spandexworld.com

ℰ Custom Printed Fabric

designyourfabric.com

spoonflower.com

ℰ Fabric

dharmatrading.com

etsy.com
(This is my favorite place to shop for fabric; I will just search the color and fabric type and scroll for ages. This is my secret weapon, so don't tell anyone!)

fabric.com

fabricdepot.com

fabricmart.com

fabricwholesaledirect.com

joann.com

moodfabrics.com

silkbaron.com

ℰ Tools

famorecutlery.com

oliso.com

sewingpartsonline.com

wawak.com

ℰ General Craft

amazon.com

dickblick.com

hobbylobby.com

michaels.com

walmart.com

ℰ Cosplay Wigs

ardawigs.com

customwigcompany.com

epiccosplaywigs.com

posewigs.com

rockstarwigs.com

wigisfashion.com

ℰ Shoes

americanduchess.com

amazon.com

poshmart.com

threadup.com

Local thrift shops are the best place for finding shoes, but be prepared to check often and hunt around.

ABOUT THE AUTHOR

Casey Welsch is from Phoenix, Arizona, and lived in Chicago for a few years, but now resides in Marietta, Georgia. Casey is a full-time business owner and entrepreneur focusing on costume and sewing education. She received her Bachelor of Arts in theatre from Arizona State University and has been making costumes for almost a decade. Casey loves traveling to conventions around the U.S., judging cosplay contests, and providing panels. She hopes to travel to conventions outside of the U.S. someday and learn about the cosplay culture in other countries.

When Casey isn't creating costumes or YouTube videos, she trains for marathons, reads books at coffee shops, and plans trips to Disney World. She loves running her business full time and giving others the power to create their costumes. She would never have learned how to sew if it wasn't for creators on YouTube sharing the information, so now she is dedicated to doing the same. Follow Casey in all her costume adventures on social media and her website.

Photography by Alexandra Lee Studios

WEBSITE: caseyreneecosplay.com ◆ **INSTAGRAM:** @caseyreneecosplay ◆ **YOUTUBE:** /caseyreneecosplay